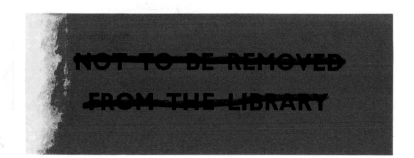

A
HISTORY OF
EVERYDAY THINGS
IN ENGLAND

Books by the Quennells

A HISTORY OF EVERYDAY THINGS IN ENGLAND
    Vol. I.   1066–1499
    Vol. II. 1500–1799
    Vol. III. 1733–1851
    Vol. IV. 1851–1914

EVERYDAY LIFE IN PREHISTORIC TIMES
EVERYDAY LIFE IN ROMAN AND ANGLO-SAXON
    TIMES
EVERYDAY THINGS IN ANCIENT GREECE

1 The Village Fair

Details of Merry-go-Round from a sketch made by Heywood Sumner in 1892

A
HISTORY OF
EVERYDAY THINGS
IN ENGLAND

Volume IV
1851 to 1914

By

MARJORIE & C. H. B. QUENNELL

LONDON: B. T. BATSFORD LTD
NEW YORK: G. P. PUTNAM'S SONS

First published, Autumn, 1934
Sixth Edition, Revised by Peter Quennell, 1958
Reprinted, 1965, 1968

Revised Edition, © Peter Quennell, 1958

PRINTED AND BOUND IN GREAT BRITAIN BY JARROLD AND SONS LTD
LONDON AND NORWICH
FOR THE PUBLISHERS
B. T. BATSFORD LTD
4 FITZHARDINGE STREET, PORTMAN SQUARE, LONDON, W.1
G. P. PUTNAM'S SONS
200 MADISON AVENUE, NEW YORK, N.Y. 10016

PREFACE

THE boys and girls for whom we write will know, from their history lessons, that as a period recedes it is much easier to get a general picture of it than of events which are quite recent. In the same way the archaeologists have discovered that the earthworks on the Downs, which are puzzling when viewed on the ground, resolve themselves into a logical plan when viewed in the air from an aeroplane. How are we to give a general picture of this period?

In 1851 our grandfathers and great-grandfathers doubtless thought that all that remained was to set the machine to work and live off its products peacefully and quietly—but the machines bred other machines, each speedier than the last, and peace and quietness disappeared. Again, the machine made more goods than were necessary to supply the local demands, so foreign markets had to be discovered; then foreign raw materials had to be taken in exchange. Unheard-of complexities and jealousies were introduced into trade. Enormous additional charges were necessary for packing, retailing and distributing.

Still the picture is there—if we have but the eyes to see it. In our attempt we have given most attention to the three great primary trades, and have shown how man fed, housed and clothed himself in these years. These are, after all, the great essentials. In the space at our command we have only been able to touch on his other activities and mention a few of the many interesting developments. We have given these in their chronological order of appearance, and if this is a little confusing then it is only like life itself in our period. No sooner had people got used to one invention than another appeared which upset the apple-cart. Our readers can search for our omissions, and then submit them to a test: Is this, that, or the other thing, an essential? This questioning is going on all over the world today, and it constitutes a revolution. We like our revolutions in this country to be peaceful ones, so if we can bring ourselves to regard certain changes as being necessary, then, with courage, we may be able to build a worthier fabric of civilisation. It is, after all, more interesting to live in a period that is alive than one which suffers from a fatty degeneration of its soul.

These are the points which we think should be remembered. We can grow all the foodstuffs we require, and mine for coal and iron. Man has invented the most wonderful production plant. With its aid he can produce all that he requires—the production problem is settled. The real question is—What do we propose to do with the plenty which Providence has placed at our disposal? It is distribution which comes to the fore now. If, as Pasteur said, "the nations will unite, not to destroy, but to build," then we can very speedily free the world from hunger and want. But if the nations continue to turn their thoughts to destruction, we shall be courting disaster. It will be said of us that we did not know how to build, and our names will be bracketed with the greatest failure in history.

MARJORIE and C. H. B. QUENNELL

CONTENTS

Kings and Political	Social
1837 QUEEN VICTORIA 1848 Year of revolutions and Chartists	1846 Repeal of Corn Laws begins Free Trade 1848 First Public Health Acts and cholera epidemic 1849 Bedford College, London, founded 1850 Ebenezer Howard born
1852 Louis Napoleon becomes Napoleon III	1852 Death of Duke of Wellington
1854–6 Crimean War	1854 Cholera epidemic Cheltenham College for Girls Florence Nightingale starts nursing
1857–9 Indian Mutiny 1859–61 War of Italian Unity	1858 Formation of Volunteers 1859 William Morris marries Jane Burden 1859–65 Mrs. Beeton's cookery book
1861–5 American Civil War	1861 Death of Prince Consort 1862 A.B.C. starts business *Unto This Last* (Ruskin) 1863 Henry Ford born
1864 Schleswig-Holstein taken by Prussia 1865 Assassination of President Lincoln Austro-Prussian War	1864 Garibaldi visits England 1865 Foundation of Salvation Army
	1868 Dulwich College (Charles Barry)
1870 Franco-Prussian War, Republic in France, and Empire in Germany	1870 Education Act (Compulsory) Ruskin Slade Professor at Oxford
	1872 Charterhouse School (Hardwick) Girls' Public Day Schools Company Girton College, Cambridge, founded
	1875 Newnham College, Cambridge, founded Foundation Grosvenor Gallery
1877 Queen Victoria becomes Empress of India	1877 Foundation of Society for Protection of Ancient Buildings 1878 Whistler *v.* Ruskin libel action
1879 Zulu War	1880 Bedford Park Estate developed
1881 Boer War. Majuba 1882 Murder of Lord Frederick Cavendish	1882 St. Paul's School, Hammersmith (Waterhouse) Death of Rossetti 1883 Foundation Boys' Brigade 1884 Foundation Toynbee Hall
1884 Grab for Africa begins	Foundation Fabian Society Foundation Art Workers' Guild 1885 Death of General Gordon
1886 Gladstone's Home Rule Bill	1887 *Looking Backward* (Bellamy) Queen Victoria's Jubilee Foundation Arts and Crafts Ex. Society
1890	1889 Great dock strike for dockers' "tanner" an hour Booth's *Life and Labour of People of London* 1891 Education Act (Free)
1895 Jameson Raid	1894 Christ's Hospital, Horsham (Webb and Bell) 1896 Death of William Morris 1897 Diamond Jubilee
1898 Fashoda incident Battle of Omdurman 1899–1902 S. African War 1900 German Navy Law	1898 *Tomorrow* (Ebenezer Howard) 1900 Death of Ruskin
1901 EDWARD VII. Boxer Rebellion	1901 Beginning of Boy Scouts
1903 Chamberlain's Tariff Reform	
1904–5 Russo-Japanese War	
1906 Self-government S. Africa 50 Labour Members returned to Parliament	
1910 GEORGE V 1911 Parliament Act	1909 John Burns' Town-Planning Act
1914–18 Great War	

Science and Industry	The Arts
	1848 Formation of Pre-Raphaelite Brotherhood
	1849 Publication of *Seven Lamps of Architecture* by John Ruskin
1851 First cable to Calais The Great Exhibition in Hyde Park	
	1853 Publication of Ruskin's *Stones of Venice*
1854 Crystal Palace rebuilt at Sydenham	1854 Holman Hunt's *Light of the World* at R.A.
1856 Working Men's College in Great Ormond St. Perkin discovered aniline dyes	1856 W. P. Frith's (1819–1909) *Derby Day* Balliol Chapel (Butterfield) Rossetti's *Annunciation* Holman Hunt's *Scapegoat*
1857 Pasteur's paper on Fermentation	1857 Wellington Memorial (Alfred Stevens)
1858 First cable to America	
1859 Darwin's *Origin of Species*	1859 Philip Webb designs Red House for Morris
1863 Foundation Co-operative Wholesale Society	
1864 London sewerage system	1864 Albert Memorial (G. G. Scott)
1865 New cable to America Mechanical vehicles four miles an hour	1866 St. Pancras Station, London (G. G. Scott)
1866 New American cable	*Alice in Wonderland*
1867 Lister at work Monier's patent for reinforced concrete	1867 Street wins Law Courts, London, competition
1869 Opening of Suez Canal	
1870 Tramways Act	
1871 Prince of Wales (Edward VII) caught typhoid fever. As a result modern sanitary system evolved by Chadwick, Corfield, Field and Hellyer	1872 *Alice Through the Looking Glass*
1874 London School of Medicine for Women Ruskin makes undergraduates build roads	1875 St. Agnes', Kennington (G. G. Scott, jun.) *Trial by Jury* ⎫ Gilbert and Sullivan *The Sorcerer* ⎭
1876 Koch begins work Bell's telephones Pelton hydraulic turbine	1878 *H.M.S. Pinafore*
1879 Foundation of Bournville Garden City	
1880 First cargo of frozen beef from Australia	1880 *Pirates of Penzance*
	1881 *Patience*
1882 First cargo of frozen mutton from New Zealand	1882 *Iolanthe* ⎫ Gilbert & Sullivan
1884 Gold discovered on the Rand Daimler invents motor engine Parsons invents steam turbine	1884 *Ida*
1885 Carl Benz builds his motor-car	1885 *Mikado* ⎭
	About 1886 Constitutional Club, London (Edis)
	1887 Competition for Imperial Institute won by T. E. Collcutt
1888 Dunlop tyre patent Foundation Port Sunlight Garden City Nansen crosses Greenland	1888 *Plain Tales from the Hills* (Kipling) *Yeomen of the Guard* ⎫ Gilbert & Sullivan 1889 *Gondoliers* ⎭
1890 First Tube railway and Forth Bridge	About 1890 New Scotland Yard (Norman Shaw)
1892 Diesel engine patented	About 1892 Beginning of Westminster Cathedral (R.C.) (Bentley)
1893 Ford's first car	1893 Utopia Ltd.
	1894 Du Maurier's *Trilby* in Harper's
1895 Röntgen discovers X-rays	
1896 Mechanical vehicles twelve miles an hour	
1897 Ronald Ross discovers malarial parasite Marconi experiments with wireless	1897 Kipling's *Recessional*
	1900 Competition for new Sessions House, London (E. W. Mountford)
	1901 Competition for Victoria Memorial won by Aston Webb
1903 Mechanical vehicles twenty miles an hour Foundation first garden city, Letchworth Dec. 17th. The Wright brothers make the first mechanically propelled flight in an aeroplane	1903 First garden city, at Letchworth, begun Giles G. Scott wins Liverpool Cathedral competition
	1905 Wesleyan Hall, Westminster, competition won by Lanchester and Rickards
1909 Blériot flies the Channel	

ACKNOWLEDGMENT

W E are indebted to the late Alan Bott for Figs. 2, 11 and 123 from *Our Fathers*, published by William Heinemann, Ltd., and Figs. 76, 94 and 111 from *Our Mothers* (by Alan Bott and Irene Clephane), published by Victor Gollancz Ltd.; and Mr. J. Jacoby for Fig. 9.

We also have to thank Mr. G. G. Garland, for Fig. 28; Hulton Picture Library, for Figs. 97, 100 and 105; the Locomotive Publishing Co. Ltd., for Fig. 106; the London Transport Board, for Fig. 117; the National Portrait Gallery, for Figs. 42 and 96; the Orient Steam Navigation Co., for Fig. 118; the Society for Promoting Christian Knowledge, for Fig. 38; the Trustees of the Tate Gallery, for Figs. 43 and 112; the late H. W. Taunt, of Oxford, for Figs. 27 and 30; Raphael Tuck and Sons Ltd., for Fig. 31; the University College Hospital, for Fig. 99; the Trustees of the Victoria and Albert Museum, for Figs. 47–9. Fig. 43 is reproduced from *Rossetti and his Circle*, by permission of Lady Beerbohm and William Heinemann, Ltd.

BIBLIOGRAPHY

Agriculture and the Countryside
Bonham-Carter, Victor, *The English Village*, Penguin, 1952.
Briggs, M., *The English Farmhouse*, Batsford, 1953.
Fussell, G. E. and K. R., *The English Countryman: His Life and Work, A.D. 1500–1900*, Melrose, 1955.
Hoskins, W. G., *The Making of the English Landscape*, Hodder & Stoughton, 1955.
Saville, John, *Rural Depopulation in England and Wales, 1851–1951*, Routledge, 1957.
Seebohn, M. E., *The Evolution of the English Farm*, Allen and Unwin, 1927.

Architecture and Town Planning
Betjeman, John, *The English Town in the Last Hundred Years*, C.U.P., 1956.
Goodhart-Rendell, H. S., *English Architecture Since the Regency, An Interpretation*, Constable, 1953.
Howard, Ebenezer, *Garden Cities of Tomorrow*, New Ed., Faber, 1945.
Savage, Sir W., *The Making of Our Towns*, Eyre and Spottiswoode, 1952.
Turnor, Reginald, *19th Century Architecture in Britain*, Batsford, 1950.

Clothes and Costume
Brooke, Iris, *English Costume, 1900–1950*, Methuen, 1951.
Brooke, Iris and James Laver, *English Costume of the 19th Century*, Black, 1929.
Buck, A., *Victorian Costume and Costume Accessories*, Jenkins, 1961.
Cunnington, C. Willett and Phillis, *The History of Underclothes*, Joseph, 1951.
Cunnington, C. Willett and Phillis, *A Picture History of English Costume*, Vista, 1960.
Manchester Art Gallery, *Women's Costume*, Man. Art Gal., 1953.

Communications
Crutchley, E. T., *G.P.O.*, C.U.P., 1938.
Kay, F. George, *Royal Mail: The Story of the Posts in England from the Time of Edward IV to the Present Day*, Rockliff, 1951.
Robinson, Howard, *Britain's Post Office: A History of Development from the Beginnings to the Present Day*, O.U.P., 1953.

Co-operation
Cole, G. D. H., *A Century of Co-operation*, Co-op Union, 1945.
Redfern, Percy, *The New History of the C.W.S.*, Dent, 1938.

Education
Argles, M., *South Kensington to Robbins: An Account of English Technical and Scientific Education Since 1851*, Longmans, 1964.
Barnard, H. C., *A History of English Education from 1760*, 2nd Edition, Univ. of London, 1961.
Cotgrove, S., *Technical Education and Social Change*, Allen and Unwin, 1958.
Curtis, S. J., *History of Education in Great Britain*, 5th Edition, U.T.P., 1963.
Hoggart, Richard, *The Uses of Literacy: Aspects of Working Class Life, with Special Reference to Publications and Entertainments*, Penguin, 1963.
Peterson, A. D. C., *A Hundred Years of Education*, 2nd Edition, Duckworth, 1960.

Food
Drummond, J. C. and Anne Wilbraham, *The Englishman's Food: A History of Five Centuries of English Diet*, New Ed., J. Cape, 1957.
Hartley, Dorothy, *Food in England*, Macdonald, 1954.

Health and Hygiene
Finer, S. E., *The Life and Times of Sir Edwin Chadwick*, Methuen, 1952.
Guthrie, Douglas, *A History of Medicine*, Nelson, 1945.
Robins, F. W., *The Story of Water Supply*, O.U.P., 1946.
Wright, L., *Clean and Decent: The Fascinating History of the Bathroom and Water Closet*, Routledge, 1960.

Houses
Dutton, Ralph, *The Victorian Home: Some Aspects of Nineteenth Century Taste and Manners*, Batsford, 1954.
Hastie, Tom, *Home Life*, Batsford, 1967.
Jordan, R. F., *A Picture History of the English Home*, Hulton, 1959.
Lochhead, M., *The Victorian Household*, Murray, 1964.
Potter, Margaret and A., *Interiors: A Record of some of the Changes in Interior Design and Furniture of the English Home from Mediaeval Times to the Present Day*, Murray, 1957.
Symonds, R. W. and B. B. Whineray, *Victorian Furniture*, Country Life, 1962.
Yarwood, Doreen, *The English Home: A Thousand Years of Furnishing and Decoration*, Batsford, 1959.

Leisure
Clunes, Alec, *The British Theatre*, Cassell, 1964.
Football Association, *100 Years of Soccer in Pictures*, Heinemann, 1963.
Hamilton, R., *Now I Remember: A Holiday History of Britain*, Chatto and Windus, 1964.
Lindgren, E., *A Picture History of the Cinema*, Vista, 1960.
Low, Rachel and Roger Manvell, *A History of the British Film, vol. 1, 1896–1906*, Allen and Unwin, 1948.

13

BIBLIOGRAPHY

Leisure (contd.)
Low, Rachel and Roger Manvell, *A History of the British Film, vol. 2, 1906–1914,* Allen and Unwin, 1949.
Low, Rachel and Roger Manvell, *A History of the British Film, vol. 3, 1914–1918,* Allen and Unwin, 1950.
Mander, Raymond and Joe Mitchenson, *A Picture History of the British Theatre,* Hulton, 1957.
Manning-Sanders, Ruth, *Seaside England,* Batsford, 1951.
Pimlott, J. A. R., *The Englishman's Holiday: A Social History,* Faber, 1947.

Libraries
Minto, John, *A History of the Public Library Movement in Great Britain and Ireland,* Allen and Unwin, 1932.
Munford, W. A., *Penny Rate: Aspects of the British Public Library History, 1850–1950,* Lib. Assoc., 1951.

Living Conditions
Bruce, Maurice, *The Coming of the Welfare State,* 3rd Edition, Batsford, 1966.
Mayhem, Henry, *London Labour and the London Poor* (4 vols.), Griffin, 1851–1861.
Webb, Sidney and Beatrice, *The Prevention of Destitution,* Longmans, 1912.

Science and Technology
Bernal, J. D., *Science and Industry in the 19th Century,* Routledge, 1953.
Clow, Archibald and Nan L., *The Chemical Revolution: A Contribution to Social Technology,* Batchworth, 1952.
Dunsheath, Percy, Ed., *A Century of Technology, 1851–1951,* Hutchinson, 1951

Social History
Adburgham, A., *A Punch History of Manners and Morals, 1841–1940,* Hutchinson, 1961.
Blythe, Ronald, *The Age of Illusion: England in the Twenties and Thirties, 1919–1940,* Penguin, 1964.
Cole, G. D. H. and Raymond Postgate, *The Common People, 1746–1946,* 2nd Ed., Methuen, 1961.
Furth, C., *Life since 1900,* 2nd Ed., Allen and Unwin, 1960.
Graves, Robert and Alan Hodge, *The Long Week-end: A Social History of Great Britain, 1918–1939,* Four Square Books, 1961.
Montgomery, John, *The Twenties: An Informal Social History,* Allen and Unwin, 1957.
Ogilvie, Vivian, *Our Times: A Social History, 1912–1952,* Batsford, 1953.
Reader, W. J., *Life in Victorian England,* Batsford, 1964.
Trevelyan, G. M., *Illustrated English Social History, vol. 4, 19th Century,* Longmans, 1960.
Turner, E. S., *Roads to Ruin: The Shocking History to Social Reform,* Joseph, 1950.

Trade Unions
Pattison, G. *An Outline of Trade Union History: An Introduction for Young People and Others,* Barrie and Rockliff, 1962.
Pelling, H., *A History of British Trade Unionism,* Penguin, 1963.

Transport—Road
Belloc, H., *The Highway and its Vehicles,* Studio, 1926.
Caunter, C. F., *The History and Development of Cycles* (Science Museum), H.M.S.O., 1955.
Caunter, C. F., *The History and Development of Light Cars* (Science Museum), H.M.S.O., 1957.
Caunter, C. F., *The History and Development of Motor Cars* (Science Museum), H.M.S.O., 1955.
Davinson, C. St. C. B., *The History of Steam Road Vehicles mainly for Passenger Transport* (Science Museum), H.M.S.O., 1953.
Rolt, L. T. C., *A Picture History of Motoring,* Hulton, 1956.
Strong, L. A. G., *The Rolling Road: The Story of Travel on the Roads of Britain and the Development of Public Passenger Transport,* Hutchinson, 1956.

Transport—Rail
Ellis, C. Hamilton, *A Picture History of Railways,* Hulton, 1956.
Robbins, M., *The Railway Age,* Routledge, 1962.
Simmons, J., *The Railways of Britain,* Routledge, 1961.

Transport—Waterways
Clowes, G. S. Laird, *Sailing Ships: Their History and Development* (Science Museum), 4th Ed., H.M.S.O., 1951.
De Mare, E., *The Canals of England,* Architectural Press, 1961.
Ellis, C. Hamilton, *A Picture History of Ships,* Hulton, 1958.
Hadfield, Charles, *British Canals: An Illustrated History,* Phoenix, 1959.
Rolt, L. T. C., *The Inland Waterways of England,* Allen and Unwin, 1962.

Transport—Air
Gibbs-Smith, C. H., *Ballooning,* Penguin, 1948.
Gibbs-Smith, C. H., *A History of Flying,* Batsford, 1953.
Taylor, J. W. R., *A Picture History of Flight,* Hulton, 1955.

THE ILLUSTRATIONS

The numerals in parentheses in the text refer to the *figure numbers* of the illustrations

THE ILLUSTRATIONS

THE ILLUSTRATIONS

2   The London Central Telephone Office, 1883

Chapter I

INTRODUCTION

THIS is a book about Everyday Things in England as they were in the years between 1851 and 1914. In it we shall discuss what people did, thought and said then at home and at their work; what they wore and where they lived, and how they got from place to place. We shall not concern ourselves with the stirring political events of the time, for these are not within our province, and anyone who wishes to read about them must turn to more strictly historical volumes. All that will be found here is a record of the ordinary, simple things that people did or used every day, with some account of how it was they came to do or use them.

Before we begin, however, we must take a brief glance at our period as a whole, so that we may see what sort of framework it made for our forefathers' lives. No one in any age can live entirely unaffected by what is going on in the world around him. The most solitary and independent individual must be influenced to some extent by contemporary laws and customs, by new inventions and mechanical changes, and by such unpredictable occurrences as wars and epidemics. These touch his life at every point. His freedom, income, personal health and comfort are all affected by them, and unless he lives on a desert island he cannot ignore them. Still more important are the prevailing ideas of the time which, even if he does not always perceive it, subtly alter the colour of his own ideas and ambitions. So, if we want to understand how our great-grandparents and their successors lived, we must have some slight notion of what was happening in their day, and of the thoughts and hopes that then inspired men's actions.

Nowadays, we tend to think that the Victorian Age was rather dull and uninteresting. Because they lacked many pleasant things we now enjoy, and were hampered by conventions that have since been swept away, we imagine that our forefathers led somewhat narrow and tedious lives. But in fact this was not so. On the contrary, the nineteenth century was an exciting time to

A . 1850~60   B. 1860~70   C. 1875

D. 1878   E. 1883   F. 1885

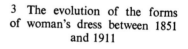

3 The evolution of the forms of woman's dress between 1851 and 1911

G. 1895   H. 1911

4   A wedding at St. James's, Piccadilly, 1862
By W. McConnel

live in, for changes were taking place on every side. It was an age of invention and discovery, when new ideas were stirring and new ways being tried out in commerce and medicine, in travel, education, and many other spheres. And, at the same time, it was a secure period, without any devastating wars or violent social upheavals, so that men could plan and look ahead in the sure hope that their work would last. We owe more than we think to those "dull" Victorians who fought to bring in reforms that we now take for granted, and to perfect inventions designed to make life easier for all. They did not always feel the full results of their work themselves, but they were laying the foundations of our modern world.

In 1851 England was a prosperous and hopeful country, most of whose inhabitants were sure the Golden Age had dawned and that henceforth they would go on from strength to strength. This happy state of affairs was one result of the Industrial Revolution, which had begun in the previous century and was now nearly complete. Trade was booming; merchants and manufacturers were making money very fast; British-made goods had a high reputation for excellence and were eagerly bought in all the markets of the world; and every mill and

21

5 An afternoon in Regent Street, 1862
By W. McConnel

factory was busy. It is true that artisans and labourers were very
poorly paid and sometimes even worse housed; but there was
plenty of work for everyone, even if it often had to be done
under conditions that would horrify us today.

In the meantime, how exciting life was for all who had a little
money to spare! So many new inventions had come to light in
the years from 1780 onwards, so many new and startling discoveries had been made, that daily life was quite altered. People
who were still young could remember when there were no railways, and "flying coaches" doing twelve miles an hour were
regarded as miracles of speed. In their short lives they had seen
gas-lamps come to the streets and even into houses; they had
seen the first electric telegraph set up in 1844, and soon they
were to see the first cable laid under the Atlantic Ocean(8).
Their parents could recall the first unreliable little steamboats
puffing over inland waters, and the excitement caused when the

22

Savannah crossed the Atlantic, partly under sail and partly by steam, in 1819. Perhaps these older people were not quite so satisfied when they remembered how many green fields had been swallowed up by ugly houses, or recalled the pleasant market towns of their youth that had swollen suddenly into dingy manufacturing cities disfigured by horrible slums(31). But many felt that this was a small price to pay for expanding industries; and it was genuinely believed then that increasing trade would bring not only prosperity but lasting peace—that the nations of the world would be united by the unhampered exchange of goods and that henceforth there would be no more wars.

Peace and prosperity based on trade was the inspiration of the Great Exhibition held in Hyde Park in 1851. An enormous glass palace, afterwards transferred to Sydenham and known to generations of pleasure-seekers as the Crystal Palace, was designed by Paxton and set up among the trees and flowers of the park. In its glittering rooms and passages every sort of manufactured product(6)—machinery, furniture, textiles, jewellery, and a host of other things too numerous to mention—were displayed before the delighted crowds who flocked every day to see and admire them. This exhibition was the Prince Consort's idea. He met with considerable opposition when he first proposed it, but from the opening day it was a brilliant success.

Not only was the great glass palace, caught in a web of slender cast iron, justly hailed at the time as a triumph and achievement of design and construction, but long afterwards it was regarded with reverent admiration by the younger school of architects as the first really modern functional building. Cast iron has been discredited by the Victorian tendency to overload its design with excessive and tasteless ornament, but though steel has mostly replaced it for construction, it is a material which is easy and fairly cheap to produce, with possibilities of an infinite range of usefulness.

True, the hopes raised by the Great Exhibition did not all materialise. Only three years later, war broke out, and British, French, Russian and Turkish soldiers fought and died in the Crimea. It did not last very long, and one good thing at least came out of it in the nursing reforms of Florence Nightingale;

6 China vase
(1851 Exhibition)

but it was enough to show that the age of universal peace had not yet come. In those days, however, war was mainly the concern of the Army and Navy, and did not affect people at home as it does today. There were no bombing-raids; there was no rationing of food or fuel; and no conscription of fighting-men and workers. Taxes and prices went up; but otherwise ordinary men and women felt little difference unless they had relations in the fighting forces.

In a way, the American Civil War of 1861 struck nearer home, though England, naturally, had no part in it. A civil war is the greatest disaster that can overtake any nation; and the twin questions of secession and slavery divided America for four weary years. The war also affected England because the bulk of the raw cotton needed in Lancashire came from the southern states of the Union. While it lasted, little or no cotton could be grown or exported, and Lancashire's mills stood silent and idle while thousands of spinners and weavers starved, or existed precariously upon relief work and charity. The result of that bitter fight was that slavery was abolished in the United States, as it had already been abolished throughout the British dominions in 1833; and to that good end it may be truly said that the men and women of Lancashire contributed indirectly by their sufferings during the cotton famine.

At the end of the century, England herself was involved in an unhappy war in South Africa; but, except for this, the time was mainly one of peace and expansion. In the various dynastic struggles that raged upon the Continent she was not concerned, though the final results of some of them were to touch her nearly in 1914 and afterwards. Nothing would have surprised the average Englishman of 1851 more than the news that his country would fight two bitter wars with Germany before the

7 Costume: mid-Victorian, late-Victorian, and sports fashions of the early twentieth century

HANDICRAFT DEPARTMENT,
KING ALFRED'S COLLEGE,
WINCHESTER.

next century was half over. Germany then, and for many years afterwards, was regarded as a peace-loving country whose inhabitants were devoted to music and the arts, and whose scientists led the way in medicine and chemistry. The English were proud to call the Germans their cousins; and if they feared or disliked any particular people, it was the French, with whom they had fought so often in the past. It is true that the Germany of those days was a collection of small kingdoms and principalities. It was not until after the Franco-Prussian War of 1870 that the German Empire was formed under the leadership of Prussia.

Meanwhile the British Empire was developing along its own peculiar lines, and offering new homes and chances to thousands of British emigrants. In the eighteenth century it had consisted of a number of colonies, ruled in some instances directly from Great Britain, and in others by chartered companies which began as purely trading concerns and ended virtually as great departments of state. But now the British Empire was beginning to take a more modern shape. In 1858, after the terrible Indian Mutiny of the previous year, the government of India passed from the East India Company to the Crown. In 1877 Queen Victoria became Empress of India, and as Emperors her successors ruled that distant land until, in 1949, it became an independent sovereign republic.

In 1867 a totally new form of imperial government began, when Canada became a self-governing Dominion, acknowledging the Queen as her sovereign, but having independent rights in her own territories. No such method of running an empire had ever been heard of before, and doubtless there were many who prophesied its failure. But one of the greatest contributions to political thought made by Great Britain in the nineteenth century was the doctrine that colonies did not exist for the benefit of the mother-country alone, but should be run primarily for the benefit of those who lived there, and that their peoples should be trained in responsibility so that eventually they might govern themselves. This fine idea was not always put into practice as quickly or as thoroughly as it should have been. Like every other idea, it had to be carried out by men who were far from perfect and who often made mistakes. But that it was sincerely entertained and excellent in itself is proved by the fact that not only Canada but also Australia, New Zealand and South Africa became self-governing Dominions.

Of all the interesting changes that took place in the nineteenth century, perhaps the most far-reaching in its effects was the great improvement in communications. We are so accustomed to travel swiftly from place to place, and to be able to get in touch immediately with distant friends by telephone or telegraph, that we are apt to forget how much more difficult such things were for our forefathers. When Queen Victoria was born, in 1819, it took four days to get from York to London by the fastest coach available. A sea voyage of any length was a considerable undertaking, not to be lightly embarked upon, and when a man set sail for America or Australia, his relations did not expect to hear of him again for months. Travelling of any kind was an expensive and cumbersome business; and, though the rich moved about a good deal on pleasure or business, simple folk often passed the whole of their lives without going more than a few miles from their birthplace.

News, too, moved slowly then. London newspapers came down by coach and were eagerly read in the provinces, even though the information they contained was already several days old. Those who could not afford them heard the gossip of the capital from the guards and drivers, and very often the first intimation of a victory or a great man's death was the appearance of the coach decorated with greenery or swathed in mourning black. Most people, however, depended upon local newssheets, which then flourished in almost every district and in which, naturally, local news had first place.

Leisured people wrote long and detailed letters to each other in a way that has gone out of fashion now. But these were rather expensive luxuries, beyond the reach of the poor except in emergencies, even if they could write. The postal charges varied with the distance covered, and were paid by the person receiving the letter, unless the writer was lucky enough to know some Member of Parliament who would frank them for him. It is said that Rowland Hill was inspired to institute the Penny Post in 1840 because he had seen a poor woman refuse a letter from her son. The charge was a shilling, and this she could not afford. He paid it for her, and she told him he should not have done so, for there was nothing in the letter but a blank sheet of paper.

8 H.M.S. *Agamemnon* laying the Atlantic Cable in 1858
From a contemporary drawing by Robert Dudley

She said it was useless for her son to write, for the postage was far beyond her means; but when he went away to work she had arranged with him to send a blank sheet at regular intervals. She always refused to take it in; but as long as it came she knew that he was alive and well. Rowland Hill understood what a grief it must be to poor people to have no real news of absent relatives; and this was one of his strongest weapons in the fight to reform the postal system.

Such was the state of affairs when Queen Victoria was born. When she died in 1901, enormous changes had already taken place and more were shortly to come. In the eighty-two years of her life the whole pace of living had been speeded up, as successive inventions and mechanical improvements made travelling, communications and trade quicker and easier. Letters now travelled over any distance in Great Britain for the standard rate of a penny, and far more people were capable of writing them. For emergencies there was the telegraph, established more than a generation ago, and cables to carry messages overseas. The telephone had been invented (2) and was being used by the more progressive business firms, though as yet it was not generally popular; and Marconi was rapidly perfecting that strange new thing called wireless telegraphy. England was covered by a network of railways which carried goods and passengers in a few hours over distances that had once taken days. Steamships plied regularly on the ocean routes; trams clanged along city streets, and that boon of the countryside, the motor-bus, was to appear in a very short time (117). Already the motor-car was making its rather unreliable way over the roads of England, a joke or a nuisance as yet to horsemen, but steadily gaining favour as its mechanism improved (116). And, in two years' time, that portent of a coming age, the aeroplane, was to make its first really successful flight at Kitty Hawk in North Carolina.

All this meant increased comfort and ease for thousands; but it also brought changes which those responsible had not, perhaps, foreseen. Life became noisier and faster. People were no longer contented with the old, quiet ways, and sought more eagerly for change and enjoyment. Annual holidays by the sea (138, 139, 141–3) came into fashion with the railways which made them possible, and towards the end of the century week-end

9 English sampler, 1874. Probably made at the Multen Orphanage, Bristol. Linen, embroidered with red silk

visits to friends became very popular. In the realm of work, too, ideas were altering. It was no longer enough for a worker to be conscientious and painstaking in all that he did; he had to be quick as well, even if this sometimes meant paying less attention to the finer points of detail.

Because of this, in the early years of the twentieth century some of the old country crafts began to disappear. The careful work of rural carpenters, lace-makers(26), quilters(25), and others, took too long; and now that the transit of goods by sea was so easy, it was often cheaper to import foreign goods and materials, even if they were not quite as good as the old native products. So it was that osier-growing, basket-making, gloving

31

HANDICRAFT DEPARTMENT,
KING ALFRED'S COLLEGE,
WINCHESTER.

10   The first car brought to England in
1888
Science Museum, London

and many other crafts that had added to cottagers' incomes in the past gradually declined. This was decidedly a pity, for the work itself was admirable, and the money earned, though it was not much, helped to make the craftsman and his family less dependent upon the low wages paid at that time. As the motor-car slowly but surely drove the horse off the roads and the tractor replaced the horse-drawn plough, once flourishing smithies (28) and saddlers' shops closed, for there was no longer enough work for more than a few smiths and saddlers in any district.

The age-old appearance of country districts began to change, too, not only because the towns were constantly spreading and eating up the fields, but also because traditional styles of building were altering. Once every district and county had its own distinctive type of house and barn, so that a stranger could tell where he was simply by looking about him. The materials used were those available on the spot, and the designs were those evolved as most suitable to the area by generations of local builders. But, now that machine-made goods travelled so easily, it was often less trouble to use standardised styles and ready-made materials from elsewhere; and if the result was sometimes an unfortunate hotch-potch of conflicting patterns that spoilt the appearance of the place and were not really suited to it, most people were in too much of a hurry to notice or to care.

And as their houses and farm-buildings altered, so did the people of the villages. Families who had lived in one place for generations, often in the same cottage and following the same trade, migrated to the cities or other rural parishes, and their places were taken by newcomers. It was no longer astonishing

32

to hear a north-country accent in the south or *vice versa*, or to see a townsman living in the country and travelling backwards and forwards to his work every day.

These shifts of population naturally brought with them new and hitherto unfamiliar ways of life. Local traditions were sometimes forgotten, because the newcomers did not know them and could not, therefore, hand them down to their children as their predecessors had done. Old customs that had been observed for centuries in particular places vanished with those who had loved and understood them, and old loyalties and ties declined as those who had been bound by them drifted away to other homes. Changes of this kind are, of course, inevitable in any age, for the essential condition of life and growth is change; but in our period they took place considerably faster than usual because they were artificially fostered by all the inventions and discoveries of the time.

If some of the alterations we have been discussing were not without their sadder side, there was one consequence of easy communications that no one could deplore. Life became wider in every sense of the word. It was not only goods and people that travelled by train and motor-car and cycle, or news alone that flashed over telegraph and cable wires. Ideas, too, and knowledge moved that way. Not so long before, a man from the next county had been regarded as a foreigner in most rural villages and was often called so. Now journeys were no longer difficult undertakings, and anyone with a little money could move about easily and see for himself what diversity of things and people his own land contained. A fresh wind of ideas blew through town and village, and what was done or thought in any part of the country was rapidly known and discussed in every other part.

And how much there was to discuss! During these sixty-three years we are considering many hitherto incurable diseases were conquered, and hospitals were made into true places of healing (99) instead of the death-traps they had formerly been. Education became available to all; the franchise was extended, and a far greater freedom and equality was extended to women. A deeper sense of social responsibility was springing up in men's hearts, and one by one the worst evils inherited from the hurried days of the Industrial Revolution were swept away. The Victorians

33

in early years were often thoughtless and unimaginative, and tolerated cruelties and injustices that seem horrible to us now (100). But they were a deeply religious people, nearly always ready and anxious to do what they believed to be right; and, once the crying need for reform was generally appreciated, they set to work with a will. So, slowly but surely, slums were cleared away, housing was improved; working hours were reduced and conditions bettered; children and animals were protected by law, and in many other directions the way was paved for the reforms of our own time.

We know that our Victorian ancestors in this period made many mistakes, as no doubt we in our own day have done, and shall do again. But they, like us, were doing their best as they saw it, and some of their best was very good indeed. If, while avoiding their errors, we can equal their courage, energy and goodwill, we ourselves need not despair.

11   Early electric lighting, in an 1882 drawing-room

Chapter II

THE FARMER AND HIS WORK

THE first and most important of all the world's industries is agriculture. Man must eat if he is to live. He can dress in skins and sleep in caves if he is driven to it; but food he must have or perish. On the day the first harvest was reaped, civilisation really began. The farmer and his labourers have ever since then formed the foundation of our world, and without their work the whole elaborate modern structure of industry, science, art, education and government would fall to the ground.

Before the Industrial Revolution, agriculture was the principal English occupation. The people as a whole depended upon their own crops and cattle for the bulk of their food. A bad harvest at home meant short commons for the poor and high prices for everybody; a series of bad harvests meant something very like famine. Harvest Thanksgivings then were thanksgivings indeed, and it was to everyone's interest to foster high production on the farms. Home-grown corn supplied the bread that was eaten at every table, home-reared pigs and cattle the meat. Eggs and chickens came from native poultry-yards, and most of the fruit from English orchards and fruit-gardens. There was then no elaborate system of importing wheat from Canada or frozen meat from New Zealand and Australia, and what England failed to grow for herself in any one season had, for the most part, to be done without until the next harvest came round.

Thus the farmer and his workers were very important people, and so were the craftsmen who served them. The farmer's corn was ground in the local mill; his ploughs and other instruments were made in the local smithy(28) and his horses shod there. His wife spun her own flax and wool for the household linen and clothes, made butter and cheese to sell in the nearby market town, and brewed all the ale needed by her family and servants. Most farm labourers had a pig and a small plot of land which they tended when their day's work on the farm was over, and their wives sometimes added to the family income by making

35

lace (26) or gloves at home, or by plaiting straw bands in traditional patterns for the hat-makers.

The surplus produce of the countryside went to feed the towns, which, in their turn, supplied such necessities or luxuries as could not be found in the villages. In this way a strong and stable civilisation was built up, with its base firmly resting on the land and its differing parts closely united by a community of interests. The country people were self-reliant and capable, and most of them had far more freedom in their work than the modern factory-hand. Landowners usually took a keen interest in their estates and sought to improve them, since they depended on them for their incomes and not, as so often happens now, upon some outside town business or on investments.

By the time our period opens, however, this age-old and necessary balance had been partly destroyed by the Industrial Revolution, which brought a disproportionate importance to the towns and made the whole structure of society top-heavy. The leaders of the industrial movement cared nothing for agriculture. They were concerned solely with the rapid expansion of industry and with the extension of foreign markets for English manufactured goods. Free Trade was their ideal, with cheap labour at home and cheap goods in the shops, and for this they were prepared to sacrifice the old ways of life, and England's ancient independence as a self-feeding nation.

In 1846 they succeeded, after eight years of agitation, in persuading Parliament to abolish the Corn Laws. These had been introduced in 1815 to protect the English farmer by forbidding the import of foreign corn unless the home-grown variety reached the very high price of 80s. a quarter. In doing this the law-makers of the time sought to safeguard the basic industry of the nation, and to protect that balance between town and country upon which all the prosperity of England had hitherto been founded. To them, agriculture was still of far greater importance than the rapidly growing industries of the towns. But to the Free Traders the Corn Laws were altogether detestable, and even when the laws were modified in 1826 they were not satisfied. An Anti-Corn-Law League was founded in 1838, and meetings were held all over the country at which it was argued that the Corn Laws not only restricted international trade but also—which was actually far more important—

inflicted great hardship on the poor whenever English harvests were bad and prices rose. This was undoubtedly true in an age when wages were very low and any considerable rise in prices a disaster for many; and it was this fact, more than any other, that eventually gained the day for the abolitionists.

The disappearance of the Corn Laws was one of the most important changes in our history, not so much because of its immediate effects as because it marked a great alteration in thought. The old notion of agriculture as mother and nurse of the nation was henceforth abandoned. Industry became the most important item in British economy instead of farming and, for the first time, political power passed from the country to the towns, so that the townsman, rather than the countryman, became the real ruler of Britain.

But if the effects of the changes were far-reaching they were also slow, and for a long time country life went on much as before. The farmer had now to compete with foreign and colonial corn-growers, and was no longer the sole supplier of the nation's food. But the population was growing rapidly, and there was still a great demand for home-produced corn, cattle and dairy goods. Farming methods, too, were slowly changing. Many improvements had been introduced during the eighteenth century, and more were to come. The inventive and progressive spirit that had already wrought such changes in the factories was not confined to the towns; and if the countryman was not always so quick to adopt new ideas as the townsman, he was always ready to do so once he was convinced that they were really good.

A large nineteenth-century dairy farm was a busy and flourishing place. Usually there were about forty cows, which were milked by hand twice a day (13). Butter was made by the farmer's wife or by a dairymaid. The milk fresh from the shippon was poured into wide, shallow earthenware pans and left until the cream had risen to the top. Then it was skimmed with a flat skimmer, and the remaining milk was given to the pigs or sold very cheaply to the village women. The cream went into a churn, which might be of various shapes and patterns. The most ordinary was the barrel-churn, a large wooden tub mounted on a stand, with long blades inside that beat the cream into butter as the handle was turned (12). Another was the "end-over-end"

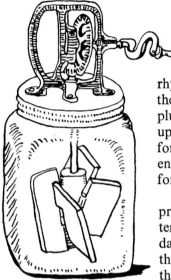

12 A typical hand churn of stationary type

churn. It, too, was barrel-shaped but had no inner blades, and the butter was made by turning it over and over with a steady rhythmic movement. There was also the upright or dash-churn, in which a plunger with holes in it was worked up and down until the butter formed. This type has gone almost entirely out of fashion, but modern forms of the other two are still in use.

Butter-making is often a slow process. Much depends on the temperature of the cream and of the dairy, and also on the cool hand of the dairy-maid, who has to press out the buttermilk, wash the butter, and shape it into pounds and half-pounds with wooden pats. Nowadays churns and butter-workers are sometimes operated by machinery on large farms; but the old hand process still goes on in smaller places. In the mid-nineteenth century it was almost universal. Churns worked by horses were used in Buckinghamshire in 1850; and a very elaborate engine from that county may be seen at the South Kensington Science Museum, in which a barrel-churn is turned by an immense spur-wheel moved round by a horse. It is illustrated in Vol. III. Such machines, however, were exceptional, and most farmers relied upon the skill and hard work of the dairymaid.

About 1879 mechanical separators came into use and the old wide cream-pans gradually disappeared. These machines worked on the centrifugal principle, and could be operated by hand or horse or by steam. The milk was poured into them at the top and came out again in two separate streams, the cream through one pipe and the skimmed milk through another. This was a much quicker and more thorough method than the old hand-skimming, and today separators of various types are found in every dairy.

Another important innovation was the introduction of

38

CHEESE-MAKING

milking-machines, by which cows are milked by flexible pipes attached to their udders. They first appeared in 1895, and proved very useful wherever large herds of cows were kept. On smaller farms they were not so readily adopted because of the expense, and even today a great deal of milking is still done by hand, unless the herds are very large.

13 Milking

In some districts cheese was a more important product than butter; and here again the farmer's wife or the dairymaid did most of the work. Cheese-making by hand is a strenuous occupation and calls for a good deal of strength, as well as skill. In one Cheshire village there is a parish chest in the church with an extremely heavy lid. It used to be said that no girl who could not lift the lid with one hand was strong enough to be a good cheesemaker; and farmers who went courting expected their future wives to submit to the test. Young women must have been very vigorous in those days, for there is no record that the local farmers had any difficulty in finding wives. Yet when we were there a few years ago, we could not find any woman who had tried the experiment and had not been obliged to take two hands to the ponderous lid.

The first process in cheese-making was to curdle the milk with an infusion of dried and salted maws of sucking-calves and lemon juice, or with a decoction made from the flower known as yellow lady's bedstraw. This had to be prepared beforehand and, in the case of the calves-maw infusion, had to be kept a year before it was used. Nowadays this labour is avoided by buying essence of rennet from the grocer, or some other ready-made preparation.

Then the curds and whey had to be separated: the curds to go into the cheese, and the whey to be made into whey-butter. The latter is hardly ever seen now, for modern methods of separating leave too little behind; but in mid-Victorian times it was a popular food in rural districts. The whey was first drained

39

through cloths, and then the last drops were squeezed out by heavy wooden presses worked by screws. These cumbersome machines have been replaced now by a system of weights and levers, which is more efficient in its effects and less laborious to use. When all the whey had been extracted, the curd was packed into tubs, and the cheeses, when ready, were put into a special cheese-room and turned at regular intervals until they were ripe.

In the eighteenth century and earlier, great difficulty was experienced in feeding cattle during the winter months. Many beasts were killed off about Michaelmas to save their keep, and their meat was salted down; the rest were left to do the best they could on whatever fodder remained for them. In the nineteenth century, however, matters were considerably improved by the introduction of linseed or cotton cake and similar foods. Towards the end of the century the process known as ensilage became general. This consists of storing greenstuff for winter use while it is still green, instead of converting it into hay. In order to preserve it, all air has to be excluded. It is tightly packed and trampled down in a silo and covered with earth or some other substance. The modern silo is usually a high concrete tower, which often has a water tank on its top to add to the pressure. The earlier silos were simpler receptacles of brick or stone, or, in some cases, just a pit in the ground. On some farms, the fodder was not put into a silo at all, but was merely built into a stack, pressed down by the weight of carts and rollers, and sometimes surmounted by an ordinary haystack to give extra weight. By the use of green foods so preserved and of cattle cake, it was possible to keep the herds in comfort throughout the winter; and this resulted in a general improvement in the stock and in methods of breeding.

Veterinary knowledge also increased. The Veterinary College had been founded as far back as 1791; but it took some time for its teachings to reach the ordinary small farm. Traditional remedies for cattle and sheep diseases, some good and some almost useless, gave way only slowly to more scientific methods; but it was during this period that the terrible rinderpest or cattle-plague was stamped out, and that great advances were made in the treatment of other ills.

In 1865 rinderpest suddenly descended upon England and

thousands of valuable beasts were lost. In a short time the cow-byres were almost swept clean of stock. Where forty or fifty or a hundred cows had roamed the rich meadows, there were often only one or two left, sometimes none at all. The farmer who left twenty good beasts in his byre overnight found them dead or dying in the morning, and there was nothing he could do to save them. The plague raged for eighteen months; and long before the end of it hundreds of small farmers were facing ruin. Good pasture-land had to be ploughed up if they were to live at all. Sheep and corn appeared in dairying districts where formerly they had been unknown. "There were no herds in the shippons," wrote Beatrice Tunstall in her fine novel of Victorian rural life,[1] "no herds in the pastures. For, even if a man could afford, of what use was it to restock while destruction walked abroad? As for the 'young things', it had grown into a maxim: Let them be slaughtered and eaten today, for tomorrow they die."

Nevertheless, this was the last great outbreak of the disease, and by 1877 it had been stamped out altogether. The Government made the immediate killing of diseased animals compulsory, and on every farm huge graves had to be dug in the fields to receive the carcases. At first every slaughtered beast meant a dead loss to its owner, but in 1866 compensation was paid at the rate of £10 a cow. The landlords also received loans from the Government with which to purchase new stock when it was safe to do so, and they advanced money to their tenants which was eventually repaid by half-yearly payments known as the Cattle Tax. Drastic as the compulsory slaughter orders seemed at the time, they checked the rinderpest and did much to prevent the spread of foot-and-mouth disease, and they also helped to stamp out a number of other ills that had seriously affected cattle in the earlier part of the century.

Horses played a great part on every farm before the days of tractors and motor-lorries. They were used for ploughing, harrowing, carting, and a hundred other necessary tasks. In the previous century much of this work had been done by oxen. Many farmers considered them better than horses, especially in districts where the soil was very heavy. Though they were slow, they were very steady in their movements; they were extremely

---

[1] Beatrice Tunstall, *The Shiny Night*, 1931.

strong and capable of an immense amount of work; and they were not easily frightened or upset. They were used for road haulage as well as for ploughing, and were harnessed to the bullock-cart by a long pole that fitted into the wooden yokes they wore on their powerful necks. For road work they were shod with an ox-shoe consisting of two plates, one for each part of the divided hoof. Their popularity declined when horse-breeding improved; but many Victorian farmers used them, particularly in Berkshire, Sussex, Wiltshire, and Gloucestershire. Ox-teams were working in parts of Sussex as late as 1914; and the last team in that county was not given up until 1929.

Carters took a great pride both in their horses and in the carts and wagons made for them by country wheelwrights. On festival occasions like May Day or the annual Wakes, carts and teams were decorated with corn and greenery, the horses wearing full sets of highly polished brasses and having their manes and tails braided with straw and ribbons. A good set of horse-brasses was often of considerable age, handed down from father to son in the carter's family and treasured by its owners. It consisted of a number of ornaments cast in the form of crescents, wheels, stars, hearts, crosses, and other traditional designs, originally intended to protect the horse from witchcraft. These ornaments were worn on the animal's forehead and on the martingale or breast-strap. There were also brass studs on the hame reins, and plates of varying pattern on the loin-straps; in some cases the blinkers were also adorned with brass plates, or with cockleshells and other designs in raised leather.

Besides the brasses there were latten bells, fitted to the hames of the collar by a hooped rod, and protected by leather flaps studded with small brass plates. These bells served as a warning of approach in narrow country lanes, where there was little room for two carts at a time. They were made in sets of four or three, each bell having its own distinctive note tuned to harmonise with the rest. Some horses also wore head-bells fastened to an upright ornament while others wore three-tiered plumes of coloured horse-hair. A well-groomed team in all the glory of brasses, fly-terrets, ear-pieces, bells, and "ridged-up" tails and manes was a very fine sight, and many carters spent hours in polishing, braiding, plaiting and grooming, before any festival or a long journey on the roads.

14   Wagon built in Dorset

Carts and wagons varied considerably in design, according to their use and the district in which they were made(14). They might have two wheels or four, double shafts or single poles; they might be built with straight, upright sides, or with sides sloping slightly outwards. Some, like the Woodstock wagon, had barred front and tail-boards; others, like the Gloucestershire hoopraved wagon, had massive wooden axles and straked wheels. In Lincolnshire and Norfolk "hermaphrodite" wagons were made by the simple process of removing the shafts from a two-wheeled cart and fixing to it an old pair of wheels from some disused cart, with a long overhanging lade in front. This useful type of wagon is still used today; but now the added parts are specially made for the purpose.

Almost every county had its own traditional type of cart, designed to combine lightness with strength and durability, and to suit the local soil and breed of horses. Great care was taken in the choice of woods for the different parts. The framework was usually made of oak, the sides, floors and wheel-naves of elm, and the shafts, wheel-spokes and fellies of ash. Every detail of construction was carefully planned by the wheelwrights to give the greatest service; and as a result many of

43

these fine old vehicles are still in use today, a hundred years or more after they were made.

Many of the older wagons were very beautiful, especially the ship-like harvest-wain, with its high harvest-gearing for holding the load in place. Nearly all were pleasantly decorated with scrolls and flourishes round the owner's name(15, 17), and on well-run farms their paintwork was always kept fresh and bright. Red, blue, and green were the favourite colours in most districts; but in some counties orange, brown, cream, yellow or stone-colour were preferred. Very often contrasting colours were used. A blue or yellow wagon might have red wheels and a red under-carriage, or lines of green, scarlet or orange might be employed to relieve a darker shade.

Road wagons were made to carry very heavy weights and had to be very strongly built. Ten quarters of wheat or a ton and a half of hay was quite a usual load for these great carts. Four or five horses were needed to draw them, and usually two or three men went with them on their journeys. Carters, who had to be out in all weathers, wore stout linen smocks, with a short cape or flap on the shoulders, and corduroy or fustian breeches. The smocks(95) were made of very hard linen which lasted for years and could withstand any amount of wet and cold. The full width of the material was gathered into folds, held together by smocking on chest and back, and thus gave extra protection against the weather where it was most needed. Sunday smocks were usually white, and were worn to church with a top hat or bowler; workaday ones were white also in some districts, grey in others, and in parts of Essex green, trimmed with blue braid.

15   Tailboard of a Somerset wagon, 1873

THE SHEPHERD

They were far more serviceable than any modern clothes worn by farm labourers, and it is a great pity that they have gone completely out of fashion today.

Shepherds also wore smocks; but theirs were longer, extending well below the knee(16). The shepherd led a more solitary life than any of the other workers, spending much of his time alone with his dog and his sheep out on the hills. Then, as now, his busiest period was during the lambing season, between Christmas and the end of March, when the weather is at its worst. His hard labour and long hours at this time were often paid for in kind, by the gift of a lamb or a bell-wether's fleece, instead of the small sum of money for each lamb which is more usual today.

16   The shepherd

At tailing-time, also, he could claim the lambs' tails, which were considered a great delicacy.

Another very busy season for the shepherd came in summer when the sheep were washed, shorn, and dipped. Sheep-shearing in Victorian times was, of course, always done by hand, as it often is today, though mechanical clippers, worked by an oil engine or by electricity, are now frequently used on large farms. Hand-shearing is very skilled work, requiring quickness and accuracy, for the fleece has to come off all in one piece, and great care has to be taken to avoid hurting a refractory or nervous animal. In the mid-nineteenth century it was still customary to follow this work by the ancient Sheep-Shearing Festival, at which a good meal and quantities of ale were provided by the farmer, and everyone joined afterwards in dancing, singing, and playing games.

The greatest festival of the year on most farms, however, was that which followed the corn harvest. It had many names. In some districts it was known as the Mell Supper, in others as Harvest Home; in the eastern counties it was called the Horkey or Hockay. Every farmer tried to get his harvest in before his

45

17 Tailboard belonging to James Kiddle, East Stour, Dorset

neighbours, and the men all shared in his enthusiasm. In Cheshire, if they finished before the next-door farmer, they went to some high ground near the boundary and shouted derisive "nominies", to the great annoyance of their rival's labourers. Then the corn was carried home with ceremony, and the Kern Baby was made from the last sheaf and hung up in the farmhouse or in the church. Finally, a grand supper was eaten by all, with traditional songs and toasts, and afterwards there was dancing.

At the beginning of our period, England was still the great corn-producing country she had been in the past; and it was not until later on in the century that a decline set in. Many people had expected that the abolition of the Corn Laws in 1846 would bring immediate ruin to English wheat-growers; but this did not happen. For years they continued to flourish as they had done in the past. But, during the course of Queen Victoria's long reign, conditions gradually changed. The great corn-growing districts of the United States, Canada, Australia and South Russia were developing rapidly; and these countries enjoyed the enormous advantage of a climate more reliable than our own. Without any form of tariff protection, British farmers found it difficult to compete against the floods of foreign and colonial corn that began to pour into England. Their difficulties, too, were increased by the fact that, in some respects, the dry, hard wheat of Canada proved better for bread-making than the English variety. Then, in the seventies, came a series of bad harvests, ending in the disastrous season of 1879; and from this combination of serious troubles English corn-growing has never really recovered.

Nevertheless, wheat, oats and barley are still very important products of our land, and in Victorian times they were grown in

46

even larger quantities than they are today. That was an age of great improvements in every branch of farming, and new machines and new methods were constantly being introduced. Ploughs were steadily improving in efficiency and design. The old simple wooden plough of former times was being replaced by the lighter and more complicated iron plough, which often had a great variety of shares and turn-furrows to suit the particular needs of particular districts. Cultivators for preparing land for sowing or for working in dressings, and drilling machines for sowing all kinds of seeds had been known at the end of the eighteenth century, and improved harrows with cast-iron rollers had been used as early as 1800.

Then, about 1860, reaping-machines appeared. The earliest type was fitted with a cutting apparatus and with a board behind on which corn was collected until there was enough to make a sheaf. When the board was full, the driver threw the corn off, and it was gathered up and bound by other workers. An improvement on this was the self-delivery reaper, which had arms like a windmill and threw the gathered corn off to one side out of the track of the machine as it came round a second time. From these beginnings developed the elaborate modern machine that cuts, binds and ties the sheaves, and finally severs the twine neatly and efficiently at the end of a complicated operation.

The early reapers were rather clumsy machines which frequently broke down; and it was some time before use and improvements made them really popular. One very natural objection to them, on the part of the labourers, was that they reduced the necessary number of workers. Many local people were engaged at harvest time, including women and girls, who followed the reapers and bound up the sheaves; and large numbers of Irishmen used to come over for the season. These men returned time after time to the same farm, sleeping in barns and

18 Reaping

47

stables on straw pallets provided for them. They were hard workers and often earned a good deal of money during their short stay; and in most districts they were welcomed not only for their help but also for their cheerful ways and their lively songs and stories.

Mechanical reapers also reduced the amount of corn left for the gleaners. It had always been the custom on English farms to allow the poorer people of the village to collect what corn they could find in the fields after the harvest had been carried(19). Many families kept themselves in bread all through the winter by this means. As soon as any given field had been raked, the gleaning bell was rung as a sign that the gleaners might enter, or some other signal was given, like the flying of a white flag or the removal of the "guard-sheaf" which had been left at the gate when the other sheaves were carried home. The local miller ground and dressed the corn for a small payment, and sometimes for nothing; and, as every cottage woman baked her own bread, she was supplied for several months at little or no cost.

But reaping-machines did not leave so much behind as workers with scythes and fagging-hooks(21); and with every improvement in the mechanism they left less. The old pleasant custom therefore declined, partly because the reward became scarcely sufficient for the labour, and partly because rising wages gradually made such economies unnecessary. It continued in some districts up to 1914; but nowadays few trouble to exercise their gleaning rights; and those who do generally use the little corn they find to feed their chickens rather than themselves.

Threshing- and winnowing-machines were first used in Scotland, and thence, during the first years of the nineteenth century, they spread slowly into England. Threshing by hand went on for a long time in this country and was continued on small farms almost to the end of Queen Victoria's reign(27). It was a very laborious process, which sometimes lasted all through the winter; but it was simple and needed no implement but the flail. This was a wooden instrument consisting of a handstaff made of ash, to which the wingel or beater, a short stick of some heavy wood, was attached by a swivel joint. The corn was laid on the threshing-floor in the barn and was beaten by a man, or by two men striking in turn, until all the grain had been separated from the straw.

When this process was completed, the grain had to be cleansed of chaff by winnowing. The simplest way of doing this was to shake it through a sieve on to a cloth, leaving the chaff to be blown away by the wind. The disadvantage of this method was that it was necessary to wait for a windy day; and, to surmount it, a wooden machine with sails like those of a reaper was introduced in the eighteenth century. One man worked the handle that turned the sails, creating a strong draught into which a second worker threw the mixed chaff and grain. The former was blown away by the draught and the latter fell to the ground for collection into sacks.

The first threshing-machines were very simple contrivances; but the principle on which they worked was the same as that of our modern threshers. A revolving drum with beaters separated the grain from the straw by rubbing the corn against a concave screen that acted as an adjustable sieve. Horses or water originally supplied the motive power; but by 1851 steam engines were already in use on some of the larger and more up-to-date farms. Later, oil engines were substituted, thereby saving the time spent in getting up steam; and these are still widely used today.

A further improvement came when winnowing-machines were added to the threshers, so that the whole lengthy process could be gone through at once. When hand-threshing was the rule, the work was done by labourers normally employed on the farm; but, with the introduction of engines, it became more usual for threshing gangs to travel about the countryside, going from farm to farm, and often doing in a single day what would formerly have taken weeks to accomplish.

Machines came late to the hayfield; and on small farms much of the work there is still done by hand. It was not until towards the end of the nineteenth century that mowing-machines were introduced; and these were followed in 1894 by a sweep-rake which gathered the hay and carried it to the stack. In the early twentieth century, elevators began to be widely used for hoisting hay or straw on to the stack by means of a revolving belt or chain set with tines. Gradually, more and more mechanical devices were added to the farmer's equipment. Tedders and swathe-turners, balers and trussers, and the now indispensable motor tractor appeared in the fields, milking-machines and mechanical separators in the dairy. The motor-lorry and the motor-car came to replace the old wagon and traps; and today a really large farm can show almost as many machines at work as a factory.

Another great change on the farm was caused by the advance of agricultural chemistry and a vastly increased interest in the science of manuring. Animal manures had always been used to enrich the soil, together with lime, chalk, marl and potash made from wood ashes. Farmers depended largely upon their own animals for the "muck", which they rightly said was worth its weight in gold; some also kept pigeons for the sake of the guano in their droppings. A variety of other fertilisers were commonly employed, such as sugar-bakers' scum, soap-boilers' ashes, hog's hair, malt-dust and horn-shavings, all of which were easily obtained from nearby towns.

19 Gleaning

Marling, for fertilising and improving the soil, was an important craft in many districts up to about 1870. The marl was dug by gangs of men who went from farm to farm, and was carted away in tumbrils to be spread over the land. It strengthened the wheat and was regarded as a valuable fertiliser; but it was expensive, and with the rise of artificial manures its use was finally abandoned. The marlers, with their elected "Lord" and their traditional rites and "nominies", disappeared, and now the only trace of their work is to be seen in the small round ponds in fields which were originally marlpits that have now become filled with water.

In 1843 the experimental station at Rothamsted, near Harpenden, Hertfordshire, was founded, and here the science of manuring was studied in all its branches. Farmers began to look further afield for their fertilisers. Potash was imported from the potash mines of Germany, and guano from the islands off the Peruvian coasts. It was found that nitrogen could be extracted from the refuse of gasworks, and that basic slag from steelworks could be made to serve the land. At first, artificial manures were viewed with deep suspicion by the older farmers, who felt that they stimulated the land too much in the beginning and left it exhausted afterwards. But, as machines slowly ousted the horse and the ox, it became impossible to depend entirely upon locally produced animal manures, and the more convenient artificial fertilisers grew steadily more popular.

All these inventions and improvements speeded up the work and enabled the farmer to produce more from a given acreage. They also lightened the labourer's toil and made him and his employer more independent of our changeable climate. But farming has never been quite the same as other forms of work; for, besides being a job to be done, it is a way of life. The benefits of mechanisation were paid for by changes that were less beneficial. Fewer workers were needed, and young men began to drift away to the towns to seek employment there. Many pleasant and ancient customs disappeared, as the work with which they were associated altered. At the beginning of Queen Victoria's reign, haymaking, sheep-shearing and harvesting in more ways than one were the highlights of the rural year. The farmer looked to them for his principal profits; the labourer, for extra pay and much cheerful bustle and jollification. Extra workers had to be taken on; the arrival of the Irishman brought new ideas and fresh company to many farms; and the hard work in the fields or the sheep-fold was followed by a feast and a host of traditional rites.

Almost every turn in the varied farming year had its particular pleasures then, as well as its labour. On some farms there was a feast after potato-lifting, and on most the ancient ceremonies of Plough Monday and other red-letter days were still observed. But with mechanisation much of this disappeared, along with the kindly customs of gleaning and "going a-Thomassing", and the traditional holidays on Shrove Tuesday and Mothering Sunday. The labourer today is better paid and freer from drudgery than at any time in our history; but he has lost a great deal that once brought colour and change to his working life; and both he and the farmer are the poorer for it.

Chapter III

VILLAGE LIFE

ENGLISH villages in the mid-nineteenth century were much more isolated than they are today, when a network of motor-buses links them with each other and with the towns, and a television or wireless set brings the ideas of the world to almost every country hearth. They were, indeed, considerably more isolated than they had been a hundred years before. The railways, spreading over the whole face of England, had driven the coaches off the roads, and as yet served few of the smaller places. There was no longer a constant bustle of traffic along the highways. Between the coming of the railway and that of the bicycle, farm carts and carriers' wagons, the farmer's trap and the squire's carriage were the only vehicles that moved regularly along the country roads. Where once the "Flying Coaches" had clattered by with jingling harness and sounding horn, bringing news and goods fresh from the cities and stirring every inn to lively activity, there was now silence; the wayside villages through which they had rumbled were left again to the peaceful quiet of their fields and meadows, as they had been long ago in the Middle Ages.

It is not likely, however, that their inhabitants minded this change as much as we might suppose. A Victorian country village was a very independent and self-sufficing place, with a decided character of its own, and indwellers who felt a strong pride in their ancient birthplace, with its cherished customs and traditions and its local styles of building and thatching. Some villages had particular crafts or industries for which they were renowned, and forms of speech that distinguished them from their fellows in other counties. Many of the families had lived in the same place for generations, and some labourers could point to a lineage as long as that of the squire, or even longer. The names in the cottages were repeated in the churchyard and the parish registers for many years back, and those who bore them often followed a trade that had been handed down from father to son from the great-grandparents' time, or earlier.

All this gave a strong sense of continuity and permanence, and produced a feeling of kinship between all classes in the village. In those pre-motor-bus days, few people travelled far from their own district; but they knew every detail of that district intimately, its fields and meadows with their individual names and needs, its woods, streams and hills, and the creatures, wild or tame, that lived in them. They knew each other thoroughly, too, and had a kindly tolerance for individual idiosyncrasy and oddity. In so small a place, every man, from the parson and the squire down to the poorest labourer, contributed something to the general life of the parish. Everyone was of value in his degree and knew himself to be so; and the result was a firmly-knit community, made up of men and women who took a proper pride in themselves and their work, and whose quiet lives were moulded by the rhythms of the agriculture they served.

20 Pit sawyers

Most of the cottages in the parish were inhabited by farm-workers of one kind or another. In some districts the un-married men lived in the farmhouse itself, very often in a wing set aside for them, with a separate staircase leading to their quarters. This arrangement had many advantages, though it meant a great deal of work for the farmer's wife and maids. Work began at a very early hour, and those who lived in were saved a long walk from the village in the cold winter dawning. They were more generously fed in the big farmhouse kitchen than probably they would have been if they had had to cater for themselves, and those who did not wish to go out at night had each other and the family for company. The sleeping-quarters provided for them were sometimes rather rough and ready, but young people are usually more tolerant of small discomforts than their elders; and, as a rule, it was not until a man's thoughts turned seriously to marriage that he began to look about for a cottage of his own.

In these days of high prices it seems wonderful to us that whole families could have been well and healthily brought up on the very low wages then paid to agricultural labourers. Many received as little as 7*s.* or 8*s.* a week at the beginning of our period; and, though the more highly skilled workers, like shepherds and cow-men, were better paid, the difference was not very great. By the seventies, wages had risen to 9*s.* or 10*s.*, and were slowly creeping upwards; but even as late as 1913 they were often not more than 14*s.* In bad years, when prices rose steeply, the average labourer had a hard struggle to make ends meet. Yet he usually succeeded in doing so, or his wife did for him; and between them they often reared a large family of healthy and vigorous children.

Such payments for good work seem scandalous to us now, but they were considered fair at the time. All manual workers were then poorly paid, and the countryman had advantages that were not shared by the men of the towns. If wages were low, so also was the cost of living. Cottage rents were about 1*s.* a week, and for this the tenant had a garden in which he grew all his own vegetables. Many farmers also allowed their men extra ground

for growing potatoes. Most cottagers kept a pig or chickens, and some bred rabbits for the table, or kept bees. It was usually possible to buy skim-milk from the farm dairy at very slight cost; and the family food supply was further supplemented by corn gleaned at harvest time. At this season, and at hay-harvest, the labourer always earned an extra pound or two, and such additional monies went much further then than they would to-day.

Fat bacon, hot or cold, was the principal meat eaten in cottages, to-gether with chitterlings, black puddings, sausages, leaf-cakes, and other fare provided by the pig. Butcher's meat was a luxury that few could afford; but an occasional rabbit brought

21 Sharpening a
      scythe

54

variety to the diet now and then. Ale, cider, mead and home-made fruit or flower wines were the favourite drinks. Tea was taken also, but it was more expensive than it is now and therefore sparingly used. Barley dumplings, with a small piece of bacon inside, were popular in some counties; and puddings made of flour and suet were often served before meat, or by themselves. Vegetable soups, with or without dumplings, often appeared on the labourer's table, for they were both economical and filling. In very poor households a rather unappetising concoction known as Kettle Broth was sometimes given at breakfast or supper. This consisted of boiling water poured on to lumps of bread and dripping, which might or might not be flavoured with a little pork or bacon, according to the state of the housewife's finances.

At festival times, furmenty was made by cooking wheat very slowly in milk until it burst, and adding raisins, sugar and spices. Bread was baked once a week in a brick oven heated by faggots. No self-respecting countrywoman then would have given her children baker's bread, which was considered vastly inferior to the home-baked loaf. Home-grown vegetables and potatoes were usually plentiful, and besides all this there was the bounty of the countryside itself—the mushrooms, blackberries, bilberries, nettles, and other wild growths, which the careful housewife gathered and used in their season to increase and vary her family's food.

Rent and food, of course, were not the only necessities that had to be provided out of the labourer's low wage. Fuel was mainly wood and cost very little. Some workers received allowances of fuel in addition to their pay; and some, like wood-workers of various kinds, had a right to the roots they grubbed up and the brush they cut away when hedging or preparing hop-poles. But clothes and shoes must often have been a difficulty, especially with a family of growing children. Shoes were made by the village cobbler; and an occasional Sunday bonnet of straw and coloured ribbons, or of black satin trimmed with rows of drawn-work, was bought from the milliner. Otherwise, practically everything was sewn or knitted at home from good materials chosen for their lasting qualities.

Countryfolk were not then greatly influenced by town fashions, but preferred to wear simple and serviceable garments

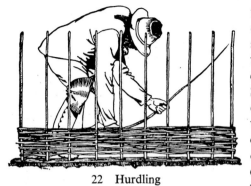

22   Hurdling

that suited their way of life. Men wore stout, weather-resisting smocks and corduroy breeches on Sundays and weekdays alike (22, 23), with a top hat for churchgoing, and an occasional spotted or coloured neckerchief to add a little variety.

Women wore linsey-woolsey dresses and thick shawls in winter, and starched pink or white cotton dresses and sunbonnets in summer(13, 19), home-knitted woollen stockings, and clean white aprons over their long, full skirts. These simple and useful clothes were easy to wear and pleasant to look at; and, as they were made of excellent materials, they often lasted for a number of years.

Many other trades besides farming flourished in the villages of Victorian England, as they had done from very remote times. Much that the farmer now obtains from manufacturers in the big cities was then supplied by craftsmen living in the parish. Every considerable village had its own blacksmith, carpenter, wheelwright and mason; it had its hurdle-maker(22) and its thatcher(23), and perhaps its saddler who made the collars and harness for the local horses, and a variety of other leather goods. There was usually a carrier who took parcels to and from the town, and sometimes also took passengers in his wide, slow-moving wagon. There might be a tailor to make breeches for those who could afford to have this work done outside the home; and there was always a cobbler who both made and mended shoes. The butcher, the pig-killer and the innkeeper were all important members of the little community; and so too was the man or woman who kept the small general shop.

The wheelwright made all the carts and wagons(14) that were needed locally, and sent his wooden wheels to the forge to have their iron rims shrunk on. When a new cottage or outbuilding was required, the local builder undertook the work, and the carpenter supplied the doors, window frames and other

56

wooden parts. The latter also made gates and fences for the farmers, chairs, chests and tables for daily use in the cottages, and coffins for those who had passed beyond the need of all else.

Before the days of corrugated iron and machine-made tiles, thatched roofs were common in many parts of England, and the thatcher was kept constantly employed (23). Thatching is a pleasant and beautiful method of roofing a house. It has the great virtue of keeping the rooms beneath warm in winter and cool in summer; and it makes them quiet at all times, for the thick covering deadens noise. Its chief disadvantage is the danger of fire; and to overcome this large iron hooks used to be hung in prominent places in the village, so that, if a fire broke out, the burning thatch could be quickly pulled down before it fell in and set light to the house.

23   The thatcher

The thatcher's materials and his style of work varied from county to county, though his actual procedure was much the same everywhere. In some parts, thick wheat- or rye-straw was used; in others, tough Norfolk or Kentish reeds. In Wales, a close, dark thatch of rushes was common; and further north, where stone or slate roofs were generally preferred, small houses were sometimes thatched with ling heather. In some areas, the porch was thatched as well as the roof, and so were the windows —a pleasant fashion which gave the effect of thick, bushy "eyebrows" on the face of the house—while in Devonshire, Wiltshire and Dorset the cob cottages often had an extra little roof of straw along the tops of the walls.

The bundles of straw or reed, known as yelms, were carefully slanted upwards from eaves to ridge, and secured to the rafters and to each other by tarred twine threaded through an enormous thatching-needle, and by double-pronged "spiks" or pegs of split withy. Along the ridge the straw was pulled over from each side and firmly woven together, so as to offer the greatest possible resistance to the winter rains. When all was finished, the loose bits were raked off, and the ragged edges trimmed along eaves and windows; and the result was a fine weatherproof roof that lasted for years and was as comfortable to live under as it was beautiful to see.

One of the most important craftsmen in every parish was the blacksmith. His forge, with its glowing fire and musical sounds of iron on iron(28), was often a favourite meeting-place for young and old, a pleasant centre of news and gossip for the elders, and a never-failing delight for the children. Here, besides shoeing, they might watch ironwork of every kind in progress. The smith made agricultural implements and ploughs for the farmers, buisting irons for shepherds to use in ear-marking their sheep, bars, hooks, hinges, and a variety of other articles needed

24   Shoeing

in the village. Sometimes he turned his hand to more ornamental work, like weathervanes, or brackets in lovely designs of flowers and leaves for the church. Many of the beautiful wrought-iron gates that are still to be seen on big estates up and down the country were made by local blacksmiths; and so were some of the finest frames for innkeepers' signs.

But the smith's most important work was that of shoeing horses (24). This called for much sound veterinary knowledge as well as skill in metals. A modern shoeing-smith who wishes to become a Master Farrier has to pass a very stiff examination in horse-anatomy and the proper treatment of foot diseases. He has to know how to treat diseased or damaged feet, and how to make and fit shoes that will allow for natural horn growth and foot expansion. In Victorian times, when horses were numerous on every farm, the smith's knowledge was even more important than it is today. Very often he was the only man in the district with any real veterinary skill; and, since a horse's health depends largely upon proper shoeing, his careful work was of the utmost value to all the farmers in the neighbourhood.

Besides all these regular trades, which were found in every village, there were some that were peculiar to certain districts. In the beechwoods of the Chiltern Hills, for instance, many men earned a living as wood-turners or chair-bodgers. They worked chiefly in the open air, or in rough sheds near their homes, making chair legs or splats or wooden bowls by means of primitive pole-lathes that had not changed their form for centuries. These lathes were very simply made from flexible poles tied with string to a treadle on the ground. The hand-riven wood was fixed on to an iron spike and made to turn against a cutting tool by the pressure of the treadle and the spring of the pole. There was nothing complicated about a pole-lathe, but it was a very efficient instrument; and a few are still to be found today in the Chilterns, side by side with the more modern automatic lathes.

In Buckinghamshire, the tent-peg makers worked all through the season in the green woods, cutting, shaping, trimming and packing thousands of pegs without any indoor work at all. In Sussex and Surrey, wooden roof-tiles were made, and in Wales milking-stools, spoons, and the wooden platters that were still used in many farmhouse kitchens. Some men made a living by shaping walking-sticks from thorn or ash branches, or by making fence-stakes and hop-poles. Deep in the heart of the woods the charcoal burner followed his solitary calling, sleeping and eating in a temporary shelter by the side of the carefully built hearths in which his logs were stacked. His fires, once lit, burnt for days together and needed constant watching to ensure a slow, even heat; and he could not afford to leave them until the work was completed. The charcoal, made from the burnt logs, was used for a variety of purposes; and it is an interesting fact that even today, notwithstanding all our modern inventions and improvements, the best charcoal is still made in the old fashion that has not changed since the time of our Saxon fore-fathers.

Clog-making was another flourishing rural industry in the days when a sound, iron-tipped wooden clog was appreciated by all sorts of workers, from dairymaids to miners. The clogger's art consisted in the proper curving of the stout wooden sole, and in applying the irons in such a way that an easy bend was given to the foot in walking. Usually the blacksmith made the irons; but all the rest of the work was done by the clogger, who split his own wood into blocks, cut the curved soles from them, applied the iron in varying thicknesses according to the needs of the future wearer, and added the leather tops. A wooden shoe seems at first sight a rather heavy and cumbersome form of footwear; but, in fact, these clogs were very comfortable, especially when they were made to measure; and they had the great advantage of outlasting any ordinary shoe, and keeping the wearer's feet warm and dry in even the dampest surroundings.

In Somerset, Berkshire, and some other counties, large quantities of baskets were made by the cottagers, who often grew their own osiers in beds rented from the farmers. Basket-making is a very interesting occupation, for it is one of the few things that cannot be done by machinery, and the varied shapes and patterns allow plenty of scope for the individual worker's fancy. There are still a number of skilled basket-makers in England, though unfortunately much of the material and many finished baskets now come to us from abroad. But in the nine-teenth century the trade was flourishing, and even thirty years ago the season for cutting and stripping the rods was almost as important in some districts as corn- or hay-harvest elsewhere. Certainly the children must have looked forward to it, since the local schools were then closed so that they might help in the work.

The rods had to be cut, stacked and seasoned in the dykes or in pits specially built for them. This done, they were peeled if they were wanted for white work, or tied in great bundles and boiled if they were to be used for the harder-wearing buff baskets. Peeling was undertaken chiefly by women and children. They used a fork called a brake, which had two iron bars joined together at one end. Through it the rod was passed twice with a rapid, whipping movement, first from one end and then from the other.

When the osier-rods were ready for use, the basket-maker pegged them into a frame and wove them firmly together into the chosen shape and pattern. His work was generally carried out at home, or in a small village workshop. He sat on the ground with his legs spread out before him, a lapboard between his knees, and his bodkins, knives, mauls and other tools all round him on the floor. Thus equipped, he made with astonishing rapidity baskets of all sorts, from ordinary garden or shopping baskets for the housewife, to fruit-carriers, turnip- or chaff-baskets for the farmer, spelks for coaling ships or lifting potatoes, and eel-traps, fish-kiddles and lobster-pots for the fisherman.

In some counties, baskets were made of rushes instead of osiers; but here the method of working was quite different. The sedge was cut about the end of June and dried for two or three weeks in open sheds. After which, the rushes were plaited together and the plaits carefully sewn into the desired shape. About the middle of the nineteenth century, Thomas Smith of Hurstmonceux invented the now famous Sussex trug, which is not woven or plaited, but made of willow cleavings fitted to a frame of split ash or chestnut. He exhibited it at the Great Exhibition of 1851, where Queen Victoria saw it and ordered several for her own use. We can imagine with what care and pride Smith made these royal trugs, but even for the Queen he was not going to trust himself to any new-fangled railway. He walked the whole way from his home to London, sixty miles or more, and, having delivered his baskets at Buckingham Palace, set cheerfully off again on the long homeward journey.

Women also had their specialised crafts, which they practised at home in the intervals of doing housework and looking after their children. Almost until the end of the nineteenth century, hundreds of housewives in Bedfordshire and Essex made straw-plaits regularly for the hat factories in Luton. Bundles of bleached straws were sent to them by the manufacturers; and with these they made plaits in different patterns, called by charming names like Brilliant, Diamond, Wisp, Shortcake, and many more. The straws had first to be split to the required size with a bone or steel tool fitted with minute blades, a tool so small that it seems wonderful that fingers roughened by house-work could ever have used it. Sevenpence or eightpence a score was paid for the simpler plaits, and rather more for the complicated Brilliant design. This may not strike us as a generous reward for such delicate work; but, even at such rates, a fast and capable plaiter could sometimes make more in a week than her husband could earn by his regular work on the farm.

No one now makes straw-plaits by hand, for machines can do it as well and faster; but gloves are still made at home in some parts of England—Woodstock in Oxfordshire, and near Worcester. Seventy years ago glove-making was a flourishing home-craft. The cut and stretched skins were sent out from the factories and sewn, pointed, finished and buttonholed by women, who could usually make fifteen or sixteen pairs a week.

SCALE OF |·····|·····|·····|·····| INCHES

25   Centre of a Devon quilt in white linen, about 1866

English heavy leather gloves are said to be the best in the world; and it is largely due to the patient work of countless cottage women that they enjoy this enviable and deserved reputation.

Quilting was done in many homes all through the eighteenth and nineteenth centuries. The quilts were made of two layers of cotton, linen or silk, with a lining of scoured sheep's wool between; and they were worked in beautiful designs of leaves, roses, shells, waves, spirals, and crowns (25). Each quilt took a long time to make, but it lasted for years.

LACE MAKING

Some of the older products of the quilt-makers are still in use today after being regularly used and washed for 150 years.

Of all the home-crafts practised by women in Queen Victoria's time, perhaps the loveliest was that of lace making (26). In some districts, almost everyone took a hand in it, and there were special lace-schools where children were taught the delicate art.

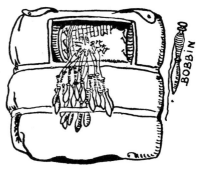

26 A lace pillow and bobbins, Sussex

In the Home Counties, it was a common sight to see a woman sitting at her cottage door with her lace-pillow mounted on a stand before her, her busy fingers rapidly moving the bobbins to and fro over a pattern pricked out with brass pins. These bobbins were small, shaped pieces of wood, bone, ivory or brass, to which the threads were attached; the lace was made by jumping them one over the other and thus weaving the threads into the design. They were often elaborately carved and adorned with mottoes; and some had red, blue and white beads, known as jingles, attached to a wire loop at one end. The simpler ones were made at home, or by the village turner. They were often given as presents, especially by young men, who made them for their girls with some such motto as "A present for my true love", or "I love you as the birds love cress", carved upon them.

Buckinghamshire and the surrounding counties were the principal homes of point lace; in the West of England Honiton and Devonshire net laces were made; and at Coggeshall in Essex a fine tambour lace that is said to have been introduced about 1810 by a Frenchman who had settled in that village. Most of the work was, of course, done in the daytime; but sometimes, if a special order had to be finished in a given time, it was necessary to work at night. Then, to save the cost of many candles, a lace-maker's light was used. This was a large glass globe fitted into a leaden cylinder, which stood on the table with a lighted candle placed near it in such a way that the rays were reflected by the glass directly on to the work.

63

In many districts, alas, this lovely craft has now almost completely disappeared—partly because it was never well paid, and
the lace-schools were closed after the Education Act of 1870;
partly because, with changes in fashion, people came to prefer
heavy foreign laces to the light and lovely English work. Today
there are still a few women here and there who make lace in
their homes, but their numbers are very small compared with
those of seventy or eighty years ago.

Apart from the enjoyable crafts in which they engaged,
Victorian villagers had many diversions; and old festivals were
still kept up that have since shrunk to a mere shadow of their
former splendour. Most parishes had a troupe of Morris-
dancers or, in the North of England, sword-dancers, and usually
there was also a team of Mummers. These were all local men
who had learnt the traditional dances and the words of the
ancient Mumming-play from their fathers and grandfathers.
They performed at certain seasons of the year—the Morris-men
at Whitsun, May Day and the Wakes: the Sword-dancers at
Christmas and on Plough Monday: and the Mummers at Christmas, Easter or All Saints. The dancers are still to be seen in
some parishes; and a pleasant sight they are in their white shirts
and trousers, with gaily-coloured ribbons on their hats and
across their chests, and pads sown with jingling bells on their
legs.

The Mummers, too, survive in a few places; but they are
fewer now than they once were. They used to go round from
house to house, crowding in from the dark winter night with a
good deal of laughter and talk, and acting in hall or kitchen or
wherever there was space for them. Everyone knew what the
play was about, for it had been acted year after year for centuries. It concerned St. George and the Turkish Knight, and was
really a sort of parable of the growing corn. But few thought of
its inner meaning as they watched the fight between the two
chief characters and saw the dead hero raised to life by the
Doctor's magic art. The visit of the Mummers was one of the
great excitements of Christmas-time.

Then there was May Day, when the children went round with
flower garlands, and a Maypole was set up on the green. A May
Queen was chosen from amongst the prettiest girls in the parish,
and there were day-long processions, dances, and a variety of

27   Threshing with the flail in Oxfordshire, about 1895

28   A smithy at Fittleworth, Sussex

other amusements. In some counties it was the custom for the May-Birchers to tour the township on April 30th, leaving branches of different trees outside the house doors. This was something more than a pleasant way of decorating the village. The name of the branch chosen rhymed with what was supposed to be the householder's chief characteristic; and what was left by the May-Birchers therefore expressed what they and the villagers thought of those who lived in the house. Thus, the fair of face or character had their doors adorned with pear; those who were admired and esteemed had branches of lime. But plum meant that the inhabitants were glum and bad tempered, and a thorn bough that the family, or some member of it, was an object of scorn throughout the parish. House-dwellers must surely have looked outside a little nervously on May-morning!

The two chief events of the village year were usually the Club Walk and the Wakes. Nearly every parish had its men's club—sometimes more than one—and often there was a women's club as well. These existed to help their members in sickness and unemployment before the days of national insurance, and once a year they held a grand procession and feast. Dressed in their best, and carrying white rods, posies and banners, the members marched first to the church, with the village band playing before them. A special service was held there, and then the whole company went to the local inn for a vast dinner of roast beef, plum puddings and ale. In one Oxfordshire village a melancholy occasion is still remembered, when the baker burnt the dinner, and the hungry clubmen, disappointed of their looked-for feast, put him in a barrel and rolled him down a stone-quarry as a punishment. In the afternoon there were games and dances, and the festivities often went on until well after dark.

The Wakes was a more general holiday, which fell on the festival day of the saint in whose name the church was dedicated. Or perhaps we should say that it began then, for sometimes it lasted for several days. It was a great time for family reunions and hospitality, when all who could invited friends and relations from other parishes; and everyone did his or her best to provide a generous spread at table. Booths were set up in the village for the sale of cakes, ale, ribbons and trinkets; cheapjacks, fortune-tellers and sideshow-owners came from the nearby towns; and every sort of jollification was indulged in, from horse-racing and dancing to grinning through a horse-collar or climbing a greasy pole to win a fat pig.

Like the Club Walks, the Wakes began with a church service; and in many districts rushes were still brought to the church, though the real need for them was gone. In earlier days most churches had floors of beaten earth or stone, and rushes were strewn on these to keep the feet of the worshippers warm and dry. They had to be changed from time to time; and it was customary to bring in new loads with a great deal of ceremony at the Wakes and other festivals. About the middle of the eighteenth century, many church floors were boarded over; so the rushes were no longer needed. But rush-bearing was too lovely and loved a custom to be abandoned immediately, and in many parishes it went on nearly to the end of Queen Victoria's reign.[1]

Every outlying hamlet contributed its quota of reeds, as well as the church town itself. They were stacked in towering piles on to decorated harvest-wains, bound down with flower-wreathed ropes, and drawn by the best team of horses the place could provide. Before each cart went the Morris-dancers and villagers carrying garlands; and on the top of the load a bower of green branches was built, in which sat a man who directed the procession. During the day the rush-carts went all round the parish, stopping outside the farms and larger houses to allow the dancers to perform. Towards evening they returned to the church, where the reeds were strewn on the floor and the garlands were hung up in the chancel and side-chapels.

Cricket and football were played on every village green, and bowls in alleys at the local inn. There were other games, like Tipcat and Prisoner's Bars, that have since been forgotten. In the winter the foxhounds sometimes met in the village, and those who could not afford to ride came to watch the start of the hunt, and might perhaps follow hounds a little way on foot. There were cross-country horse races too, in which the farmers' sons took part, and big shoots for the landlords where the labourers often earned extra money as beaters. Ratting and rabbiting were also popular sports; and now and then there was a Penny Reading in the school, a form of entertainment that was then much enjoyed in the country.

[1] See Christina Hole, *English Custom and Usage*, 1948.

No account of rural life would be complete without some mention of the annual Fair(1, 29). This was held as a rule in some market town or small borough, usually in autumn, but sometimes in the spring or early summer. Everyone looked forward to it, but not only for the pleasures it provided. In medieval times, fairs were the great trading occasions of the year, when huge quantities of goods were bought and sold, and hundreds of pounds changed hands. By the nineteenth century they had declined in importance, but cattle, horses, pigs, corn, cheese and cloth were still sold there, and dealers from all over the country found it worth their while to come with their goods.

All sorts of other people came as well—gypsies and show men, quack doctors selling nostrums said to cure every ill, "fat ladies", men with dancing bears, tumblers, and every kind of entertainer. The din was appalling, what with the music of hurdy-gurdies and roundabouts, the shouts of sellers and side-show-owners, the lowing of cattle and the thudding of horses' hooves; but that only added to the fun for those whose lives were mostly passed in quiet places.

29   Greenwich Fair, about 1850
By Richard Doyle

30 A hiring fair at Burford, Oxfordshire, about 1885

31 Mills and dwellings, Colne, Lancashire

The Hiring or Mop Fairs were important to young people in another way(30). At these they sought new places, and farmers and their wives came to look for new labourers and indoor servants. Those wanting employment stood in a long row, with some mark of their calling about them, so that everyone could tell at a glance what their work was. Shepherds wore a tuft of wool in their hats or carried a crook; carters carried a whip, and dairymaids a milking-stool or pail. Engagements then were made by the year in most districts; and, when the bargain had been duly struck, the workers received a "fasten-penny", or earnest money, usually a shilling. Then, the important business of the day being done, they went off to enjoy themselves. A few weeks later a Runaway Mop Fair was often held in the same place, in order to give a second chance to those who, for one reason or another, had already left their new employment. This system of engaging farmworkers and servants has disappeared now, and we hear no more of Hiring Fairs; but all through the nineteenth century they were quite common, and some even went on as late as 1905 or 1906 before they were finally abandoned.

Chapter IV

TOWN AND COUNTRY BUILDING

THE art of building graceful and dignified houses of all kinds came into full flower in the eighteenth century. In that cultivated and leisurely age, architecture was not regarded as the province of the architect alone. All well-educated men were expected to have some slight knowledge of it, and some acquired a great deal; the majority were quite capable of giving advice upon the building of their homes, and one or two designed them throughout themselves. To possess a good, substantial dwelling, large or small, was the ambition of every man with a little money to spare; and, as a rule, he knew exactly what sort of a house he wanted and saw that he got it. Changes in design and easier ways of transporting materials encouraged the erection of new buildings everywhere, or the alteration of old ones; and much fine work was done at this time, sometimes by qualified or amateur architects, and sometimes by master-builders and master carpenters who worked according to their own plans.

The ordinary house of the period was a simple, soundly built structure of brick or stone, with finely proportioned rooms, graceful staircases, and well-made doors and windows. It was pleasing to the eye and excellently fitted to its purpose. Some of the larger mansions were perhaps more splendid than convenient, and rather too like palaces to be altogether comfortable as homes; but the smaller dwellings were all that any home-maker could desire. Their furniture was dignified and pleasant, and there was not too much of it; the sitting-rooms were spacious and airy, the kitchens large and usually supplemented by pantries, china-closets, washhouses and other offices. There was plentiful storage space, which always makes housekeeping easier; and, in the wealthier establishments, there was ample stabling and a number of useful outbuildings.

Small rural cottages were naturally less convenient; but here too the same good rules were followed. Singly or in pairs, they were soundly built of local materials. The kitchen formed the

71

centre of the home, with a back-kitchen or scullery behind; usually there was a parlour as well, and nearly always an outhouse for stores. Two or three bedrooms completed the house; and outside there was a fair-sized garden in which the householder could grow his own flowers and vegetables.

It is true that cottages then, and for long afterwards, lacked many amenities that we now consider essential for comfort. They had no indoor sanitation, and all the water had to be drawn from wells, which in some cases meant carrying it from a distance. Ventilation was not greatly appreciated at that period, and not all the windows were made to open. The stairs were often steep and ladder-like, and the bedrooms frequently lacked ceilings and lay directly under the rafters. But people rarely feel the need of amenities to which they are not accustomed; and the cottages themselves were neat and comfortable, like the larger houses of the day; and with their thatched or tiled roofs, their walls of local stone or brick, and their bright flower-filled gardens, they fitted into their surroundings as harmoniously as a natural growth.

The tradition of good building and planning was so firmly established in the eighteenth century that it seems strange it should ever have been forgotten. But houses and streets, like clothes, express the mood of their time; and, when the mood changes, fashions in building follow suit. The nineteenth century saw great alterations in this as in so much else, and not all these alterations were for the better.

It was at this period that the towns began to expand in a hurry, with all the disadvantages that doing things in a hurry often brings. The Industrial Revolution, which began in the late eighteenth century, was by now well under way, and the whole balance of life and work was changing. Up to this time, as we have seen, England had been mainly an agricultural country. Now, however, she was becoming an industrial nation, and entirely new conditions were being created. Where formerly spinners, weavers and other artisans had worked at home in their cottages, or in a few small country mills, they now began to congregate round the larger factories, and to move from rural districts to the towns. Many Irishmen also migrated to England in search of steady work, and thousands found employment in

72

the new mills and factories that were springing up everywhere in the North and Midlands.

All these people had to be housed somehow; and "somehow", unfortunately, more or less describes what was done. Perhaps "anyhow" would be a better word. There were then no building regulations or restrictions; and in that hurried age the old ideals of town-planning were altogether forgotten. Row upon row of hideous dwellings were hastily run up(31). Mean streets and airless courts developed like mushrooms. In mining districts depressingly ugly villages appeared, where grimy houses huddled together round the pit-head, under the dark shadow of the towering slag heaps. The fields round every manufacturing town were covered by dreary buildings; and the townsman, to whom those fields had been as familiar as his own cobbled thoroughfares, suddenly found himself entirely cut off from all the rural pleasures in which he had formerly delighted.

All this was bad enough; but it was not the worst. Widespread ugliness is a high price to pay even for regular employment; but at least it would have been something if the new houses had been convenient and well built. Unhappily, they were not. They were small, dark and ill-planned, and only the cheapest materials were used in their construction. Some were back-to-back houses, with no intervening space in between; so that a through current of air was impossible, and unhealthy conditions existed from the start. They were often grossly overcrowded. Often several families huddled together in a house barely large enough for one, and some were forced to live in cellars below the level of the ground.

Little attention, moreover, was paid by the builders to means of rubbish-disposal or the provision of an adequate water-supply. With so many people herded in insanitary courts and narrow streets, rubbish accumulated very fast. The existing wells and pumps were far too few for all the families who wished to use them, and the sanitation was of the most primitive type. It must be remembered that such conditions—just bearable in the country, where there is space and fresh air—become dangerously unhealthy in a crowded town; and it is not surprising that infectious diseases, like typhus, cholera(103) and small-pox, constantly broke out in the early years of the nineteenth century.

This was the beginning of the slum problem, with which Members of Parliament and town councillors have been trying to grapple ever since, and which even today has not been entirely overcome. Congestion, bad arrangements, poor materials and insufficient water will reduce any house to the level of a slum in a very short time; and some of these new houses became slums almost as soon as they had been finished. It is hard, indeed almost impossible, to keep a home clean when there is only one water tap for a whole court; it is harder still to lead a decent life, and bring up children properly, in a house too small for the family it contains. Some of the dwellings in the northern manufacturing towns were quite unfit for human beings to live in, and it is small wonder that their inhabitants often took refuge in the alehouse or the gin shop.

It was not artisans' cottages alone that suffered from the spreading blight of ugliness. In their own way, many larger houses(32) and public buildings were equally deplorable. Here it was not excessive economy or poor materials that was to

32   Ettington Park, Warwickshire, 1858
J. Prichard, of Llandaff, Architect

74

blame. The Victorians, like the Elizabethans, loved splendour and magnificence, but, unlike the Elizabethans, they had very little taste. Or perhaps it might be said of them that they had "plenty of taste and all of it bad". What they chiefly admired was profusion in everything and a heavy form of comfort. They had a passion for the "picturesque" and the "romantic", but they lacked restraint and a sense of fitness; and the result of their work, therefore, was not the rich beauty for which they had hoped, but vulgarity and clumsy ostentation.

33 A cast-iron capital, with applied ornaments: the Parks Museum, Oxford

Houses became fussy, complicated and over-ornamented; streets were a jumble of all sorts of styles, their lines broken by a medley of bay windows, Gothic porches, turrets and other fanciful additions (33). Extensions to towns were no longer planned as a single architectural unit; and no effort was made to preserve the old relation between city and country.

Spreading suburbs engulfed the nearby villages and swallowed up farm and field so rapidly that, as Charles Eastlake wrote in 1868: "No one need be surprised to find the meadow-land which he walked in spring laid out in populous streets by Christmas."[1] Little boroughs began the evils of what we now call ribbon development by putting out tentacles in the shape of elongated roadways stretching beyond their old boundaries towards those of their neighbours. In time, these creeping streets, with a flock of side streets behind them, reached out to join those of the next township; so that today in some districts —for instance, between Preston and Warrington—it is possible to drive for thirty miles or so through an almost continuous double line of houses.

Even the remoter country areas were affected by the general lack of a sense of fitness. Rural builders hitherto had depended upon local materials and local traditions, and consequently

[1] Charles Eastlake, *Hints on Household Taste*, 1868.

there was a pleasingly individual character about every English village. Now, however, materials of all sorts were abundant and easily transported from place to place by rail. The old regional styles began to disappear and were replaced by commonplace urban notions. For the first time, red or yellow brick houses sprang up in the midst of grey stone villages; and slates or cheap pink tiles appeared in counties where thatched roofs had formerly been usual.

Nor were the public buildings of the period any better than the houses. They were usually of Gothic or Classical design, the first based on medieval conceptions and the second on Greek ideas. Both these styles had been known in the eighteenth century; but since that age of great builders there had been a lamentable decline in planning and execution. The new town halls, schools, railways stations and hotels were often a hotch-potch of turrets, battlements and small pointed windows, if they were of Gothic pattern, or a muddle of columns, cornices, pediments and architraves if they were of the "Free Classic" school.

"Gothic" and "Classical" architects were sharply divided into two opposing camps; and a regular "battle of the styles" raged all through the early years of Queen Victoria's reign. All these battlemented and turreted railway stations, these mock-classical town halls, and such curious erections as the Albert Memorial, seem hideous to us now; but to the Victorians they were beautiful. This was an age when trade was expanding rapidly. England was the principal commercial country of the world; and her people were quite certain that their feet were firmly planted on the road of progress. They had no doubt that, in architecture as in everything else, their achievements were in every way superior to anything that had gone before.

The town houses of this period were often tall and narrow, with four or five storeys linked together by steep and rather dark staircases, and a basement kitchen beneath. Well-to-do people considered numerous rooms to be a mark of good standing; but the rising cost of land forced them to economise in ground space. The houses therefore expanded upwards instead of side-ways, with less spacious stairs and somewhat smaller rooms than had formerly been fashionable. The servants' quarters were often cramped and awkward, both for working and for sleeping.

34   A garden party at the Red House, Bexley, Kent, 1860
Philip Webb, Architect

There was no room for numerous offices, as of old; and this meant that all the household tasks, once comfortably spread over stillroom, wash-house and bakery, had now to be done in the underground kitchen and scullery. All the food, coal and, where there was no bathroom, hot water had to be laboriously carried up from the basement, and the general work of the household was made much harder than it need have been by the many stairs and narrow passages.

This is not to say, of course, that all houses built then were ostentatious or ill-planned. There are few things more charming than the square white Victorian country house, with its long windows and green-painted iron verandah, or some of the pleasant town dwellings built by Norman Shaw and other architects of the day. Such houses usually had ground-floor kitchens that were as good as any room in the place; they had gracious sitting-rooms and ample domestic offices, and were both comfortable to live in and easy to run.

The Red House at Upton, which Philip Webb designed for William Morris in 1859, was an excellent building that became famous in the annals of architecture, and was to be imitated many times in the years that followed (34, 59). In its day it was

77

looked upon as something entirely new, and not everyone admired it. Morris himself was often considered a crank, and some people thought his house as peculiar as its owner. In fact, it was a solid English house of warm red brick, with thick walls and a high-pitched tiled roof, set in a pleasant garden full of apple trees. Its rooms were simple and well arranged, with the kitchen placed near the dining-room so as to save unnecessary work and ensure that the food came hot to the table. Like many other buildings of that period, it drew its inspiration from the past; but it differed from the usual Gothic structure because it was neither fanciful nor over-ornamented.

Philip Webb may be considered a decided pioneer. But, even at the beginning of our period, George Devey, who deserves to be better known and remembered, had designed some pleasant domestic work in which something of the spirit and qualities of English traditional building was carried on; his Post Office and cottages at Penshurst are dated 1850. But the architect who did more to raise house design to a higher level of sanity, effectiveness and good proportion was Richard Norman Shaw. In 1874 he built Lowther Lodge, now the home of the Royal Geographical Society; and in 1879 he published the designs for Bedford Park, which seems to have been the private venture of Jonathan Carr, a London cloth merchant. This was an early experiment in garden-city building, and its houses continue to stand up well.

Bedford Park is also interesting because it marks the combination of Renaissance detail with nineteenth-century architectural design. By 1888 Shaw was designing 170 Queen's Gate, near the Imperial Institute, South Kensington, which was built for Mr. White, the manufacturer of Portland Cement. It has sash windows, with a good cornice and a hipped roof. In fact, Shaw had returned to the real Later Renaissance architecture which we associate with Queen Anne and Sir Christopher Wren. It is very interesting that one man should have reflected the development of two or three centuries of English architecture. Shaw's Grimsdyke, Harrow, shows him as a Goth (35); his house in Fitzjohn's Avenue is neo-Jacobean in character, and 170 Queen's Gate distinctly Later Renaissance.

With Norman Shaw was associated Ernest Newton, who produced a large number of excellent country houses in the course

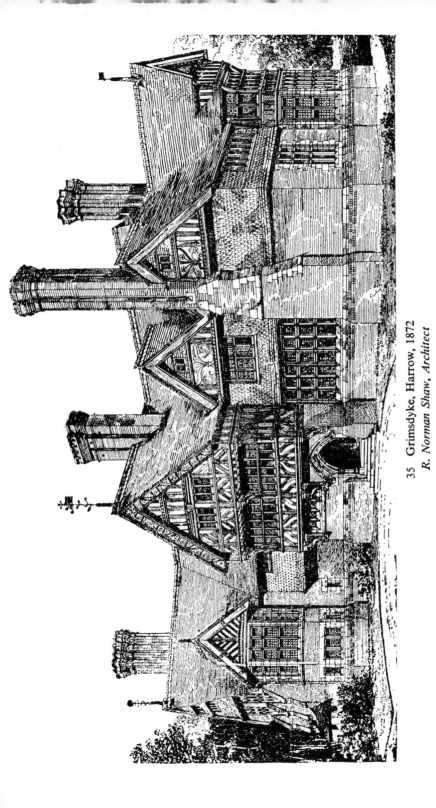

35 Grimsdyke, Harrow, 1872
R. Norman Shaw, Architect

of many years. Thus the revival of domestic architecture was firmly established; but we have not space to describe the work of many other excellent designers, such as Sir Guy Dawber and Baillie Scott. Most prominent and famous in the latter part of the nineteenth century was Sir Edwin Lutyens, whose work perpetuates the qualities of the English vernacular style, with a version of Free Classic for urban building. Mention should be made of the work of C. F. A. Voysey, who for some time was an assistant of George Devey. We illustrate a typical house designed by him about 1900 (40). This has a remarkably modern quality and, like all his later work, has not yet begun to date. To illustrate how prices have increased, we should explain that a house of this type was built for about £600. C. R. Mackintosh, who designed the Glasgow School of Art in 1894, and George Walton, who did the early Kodak shops in London, may be instanced as other pioneers in the modern movement; and a fourth was Edgar Wood.

The two-thirds of a century of our period was a tremendous time for the building of new churches and the restoration, mostly unhappy, of countless old ones. We refer to the Battle of the Styles (Classic *v.* Gothic); and, while Gothic had won for all

36 The original store of the Rochdale Pioneers, now a Co-operative Museum

ecclesiastical buildings, it is curious to note that in 1856-7 Alexander ("Greek") Thompson designed and built a church in Caledonia Road, Glasgow (37), in a severe and effective version of Greek. The Gothic revival had by 1850 been through several earlier phases—mostly a reproduction of the Perpendicular style of the fourteenth and fifteenth centuries, of a rather thin and wiry character. This work commends itself warmly to some contemporary architectural writers—probably more than its deserts warrant. A.W.N. Pugin (1812–52) had worked himself to death by 1852. But his influence continued; and the most

37 Caledonia Road Church, Glasgow, 1856
"Greek" Thompson, Architect

prolific and prominent architect of the period was Sir George Gilbert Scott (1811–78), who erected an enormous number of well-proportioned, but generally mechanical and lifeless, Gothic buildings which afforded him a high measure of satisfaction, not shared by critics of the present day. Typical examples of his work may be seen at St. Mary Abbots', Kensington, and St. Giles, Camberwell. George Edmund Street (1824–81) also produced a large number of churches of rather similar quality, and with the same limitations, such as St. Mary Magdalene,

81

Paddington, and SS. Philip and James, Oxford. He died of overwork on the ill-starred London Law Courts. The prevailing style of these two and their contemporaries was the Early English of the thirteenth century, which was regarded as the purest and best Gothic. James Brooks was another prominent designer in the Early English style, who erected a number of churches, many in brick, of which the best is the Good Shepherd, Gospel Oak. William Butterfield (1814–1900) specialised in polychromatic brickwork and other materials, as at Keble College, Oxford. In All Saints', Margaret Street, London(39), there is scarcely a square inch that is not covered with some coloured pattern, whether in brick, granite, marble, alabaster or painting, mosaic, stained glass and gilding. It was highly praised in its day, but to the twentieth-century observer it suggests a faded Jezebel. The emancipation from these hard mechanical productions was started by George Gilbert Scott the Younger, at St. Agnes', Kennington, in 1875(38); and G. F. Bodley (1827–1907), with whom was associated Thomas Garner, carried on this development, basing their designs, like the younger Scott, on the Decorated work of the fourteenth century; their churches may be seen at Clumber, and Holy Trinity, Kensington Gore. A still abler and more original designer was John D. Sedding, whose striking and attractive Holy Trinity, Sloane Street, London, has now been repaired after bomb damage. The design for Liverpool Cathedral, worked out over a number of years by Sir Giles Gilbert Scott, grandson of Sir George Gilbert, is impressive and original, and shows how far church work had progressed since the competent but unimaginative earlier imitative work, such as J. L. Pearson's Truro Cathedral (1880–7); at St. Augustine's, Kilburn, and St. John's, Red Lion Square (bomb-damaged), he is more individual.

The Red House, and some of the other buildings designed by prominent men, were signs of the times. We have seen that, even in the worst period of Victorian architecture, there were a few people who resented the prevailing ugliness and set out to achieve something better. As early as 1860, a reaction set in against the haphazard building of ill-planned dwellings for artisans in the manufacturing towns. Far-sighted men rightly felt that decent modern families should not be housed in what were little better than hovels, and towns should not be

82

38   St. Agnes', Kennington,
London, 1875
George Gilbert Scott, junr.,
Architect

39   All Saints', Margaret
Street, London, 1850
William Butterfield,
Architect

40   House at Limpsfield, Surrey, about 1900
C. F. A. Voysey, Architect

disfigured by detestable rows of mean and insanitary streets. Nor
were individual roads and houses the only things that needed
attention. Public parks, and, if possible, space for gardens, were
necessary if the inhabitants of large cities were not to be
altogether cut off from natural sights and sounds; belching
smoke from factory chimneys must somehow be abated, and
good drainage and ample pure water must be supplied.

Many of these notions are commonplaces to us now; but it was
the work of the Victorian reformers that made them so. In 1864,
Octavia Hill began what was later to develop into a world-wide
movement. She had already done much good work among the
London poor, which had taught her that many of the faults of
the poor were simply due to bad housing. It was idle, she felt,
to expect women to be clean and orderly if their houses were
filthy, verminous and insanitary. Nor could children be kept off
the streets, and be properly brought up, when home was so
uncomfortable that almost any other place was preferable. In
such conditions the most self-respecting tenants were apt to
become dirty and careless; and the house-owners, seeing this,
felt that it was useless to improve their property.

Thus a vicious circle was set up; and a great deal of courage and persistence was required to break it. Octavia Hill possessed both these qualities in good measure, together with a kind heart and much sound, practical common sense. She bought three houses, all inhabited, and all of them in a shocking condition. The drains were blocked, the water supply was out of order. The paper was hanging in strips from the filthy walls, and fittings of all sorts, from door handles to windows, were broken. The sights and smells and general air of hopelessness were enough to daunt anyone less determined than Octavia. And certainly it did not seem likely that she would get much support from the discouraged women who inhabited them.

She began by spending part of her money in making the houses habitable, and by setting the rest aside to keep them so. She made friends with the housewives and encouraged them to take a pride in their homes. She visited them every week, listened to their suggestions and complaints, attended to small repairs immediately, and introduced larger improvements as quickly as possible. "Rent-day" ceased to be a dreadful occasion, though she insisted that all rents must be punctually paid. The women came to look forward to her visits and to showing her small changes for the better that they had made themselves since she was last there. For the first time, perhaps, they felt they were dealing with someone who really understood their difficulties and—what was even more important—treated them as responsible human beings. In spite of all that pessimists had had to say, they responded at once to her encouragement; and in a very short time the houses were improved almost beyond recognition. What interested the outside world in this experiment was the fact that it was a financial, as well as a moral, success. Octavia Hill, from the first, insisted on running her property on a business basis. In her view, hers was a work not of charity but of common sense; if the tenants benefited materially and spiritually, so did the landlord. That this was indeed so, she proved conclusively with her first three houses and, later on, with others that she bought and ran in the same way.

As time went by, other landlords began to seek her advice and follow her example. In 1884, the Ecclesiastical Commissioners asked her to manage their Southwark property for them. This she did with great success, showing that what had been done on a small scale could also be done on big estates. Thereafter, other organisations and city councils desired to have their property managed. It was thought that this was definitely something that women could do better than men; and a number of women came to Octavia Hill for training. Her pupils carried her ideas all over Great Britain, and eventually to various European countries and to America; and today her system of management, which began with three small dwellings in a London slum, is known and practised throughout the world.

In the meantime, the good work went on slowly but steadily in other directions. Constant agitation in Parliament and outside produced Health Acts to enforce better sanitation and the removal of rubbish. Individual builders like Thomas Cubitt laid out building estates with wide roadways and trees planted between the houses. The more thoughtful factory owners perceived how important it was to provide good dwellings for their workers, and undertook to build them. In 1879, Bournville was founded, and nine years later Port Sunlight. These were model townships attached to particular factories, and laid out on the lines of traditional English villages (41). They were not perfect, but they were as different from the old congeries of squalid buildings as gold is from lead. Then in 1898 Ebenezer Howard

41 Cottages in Queen Mary's Drive, Port Sunlight, Cheshire
J. L. Simpson, Architect

published a book called *Tomorrow* that was to have a lasting effect on the building and town-planning of the future.

Howard's idea was that people ought not to be herded together in vast sprawling towns, nor should workmen be forced to live in outlying suburbs a long way from their work. He proposed a new type of town which he called a garden city. This was to be small enough for a real social life, and large enough to contain workshops and factories. It should be surrounded by a green belt of agricultural land, and it should never be allowed to spread unduly as the older manufacturing towns had done. The houses should be sufficiently near the factories to avoid long daily journeys; the public buildings should all be grouped together in a central park, round which an arcade of shops would run. The town itself should not contain more than 30,000 inhabitants, and there would be another 2,000 people or so living in the farms and cottages of the agricultural land outside.

As a direct result of Howard's book, the first garden city was built at Letchworth in 1903. Much careful thought went to the construction of this pioneer settlement. For instance, the factories were set on the north-east side of the town because the prevailing winds, which in that region are from the south-west, would blow the smoke away from the houses, instead of over them. No more than twelve houses were allowed to the acre, and all had gardens; the roads were lined with trees, and there were plenty of open spaces and playing-fields. Letchworth did not follow Howard's original plan in every detail. Alterations had to be made to preserve Norton Common, and also the ancient Icknield Way which ran close by; but the underlying conception of a self-sufficient, healthy district, with an interdependent town and countryside, was successfully retained.

Howard's influence was widely felt both in his own time and later. We see it still in modern housing estates and model villages, as well as in the suburbs of many cities. Hampstead Garden Suburb was begun a few years after Letchworth; and in 1919 Welwyn Garden City was founded. These, like Letchworth, were definitely planned settlements, but there were also many so-called garden cities devised by speculative builders who were quick to see the advantages of this new mingling of town and country ways. They laid out their estates on rather more spacious lines than formerly, with larger gardens, more trees along the roadsides, and houses more cottage-like in character; and then they cheerfully labelled the results with the now fashionable, but in this case mis-applied, name of garden city.

In the early years of the twentieth century, a new kind of romantic architecture came to the fore. It was inspired partly by the old Victorian love of the picturesque, which now broke out in another form, and partly by the teachings of William Morris, whose personality and achievement will be dealt with in our next chapter. What he aimed at was a return to the old high standards of craftsmanship which had flourished in the Middle Ages. Unfortunately, however, Morris's work produced a host of cheap imitations, which were as essentially false to his ideals as the turrets and battlements of Victorian Gothic had been to those of the medieval builders. It was almost inevitable that it should do so. Morris hated machines and believed, quite rightly, that working by hand is a much better thing than mere machine-minding, and far more satisfying to the worker. But in the heyday of craftsmanship the population had been small. The craftsmen could supply all that was needed, and there was no competing machinery to turn out goods more quickly and cheaply. In Morris's time this was no longer true. For good or for evil, the machine had come to stay, and the population had grown so enormously that no band of craftsmen, however hard-working, could hope to produce enough for everybody.

A flood of so-called hand-made goods poured out of the factories to supply the wants of those who admired the new ideas but could not afford to have them carried out in the old, slow, careful and costly fashion. An antique effect was consciously aimed at in architecture and furnishing. Substantial villas were built to look like overgrown cottages. Many larger houses aped the famous Red House, though the reproductions were often spoilt by incongruous additions or alterations. Wooden slats nailed to the fronts of houses imitated ancient timber-framing. Small casement windows with leaden panes became fashionable, and "bull's-eyes" were sometimes introduced into window-glass, thus copying at some expense what had originally been a fault in the work of early glassmakers. Further confusion was often produced by a mixture of styles—Tudor, Stuart, Georgian or Regency—in the furnishings of the different rooms.

PLEASANT AND SERVICEABLE HOMES

Despite all this, there was a lightness and gaiety about Edwardian homes that had been unknown in the preceding century. The Edwardians did not take themselves quite so seriously as their parents had done. They preferred cheerfulness to magnificence; and if their smaller houses were often less solidly constructed, they were in many ways more convenient. There was less ostentation and more airiness; the kitchen moved up from the basement, and there were fewer long passages and dark corners. White paint largely replaced the sober hues of earlier years. In the gardens, dank shrubberies disappeared to make room for flower-beds, and there was a pleasant fashion for flower-filled window-boxes which added to the gaiety of streets. Many houses had glassed-in verandas or lobbies that served as miniature sun-parlours; and everywhere there was a growing appreciation of the virtues of light and fresh air.

In general, the houses built at this period were cheerful and comfortable, and in this they reflected the spirit of the age. King Edward's reign was a happy and prosperous time, untouched as yet by the shadow of war and the many great changes that were to follow. Life was still secure, as it had been in the nineteenth century; but it was much gayer, and there was a pleasant feeling of freedom and adventure everywhere. After the 1914 War there were to be many alterations, some good and some bad. Perhaps few among them would have startled our forefathers more than the bleak and comfortless-looking boxes that were built as homes between 1918 and 1939, or the extraordinary notion then preached by well-known architects that "a house is a machine for living in". The Second Great War mercifully checked the spread of these essentially un-English houses, which are totally unsuited to our cold and variable climate and break with all our traditions.

Today we enjoy a more comfortable fashion, even though restrictions and shortages make building more difficult than at any time in our history, and force far too many people to live, at least temporarily, in overcrowded conditions. But that is a subject for another book. In the meantime, we can look back with gratitude to the great Edwardian architects who, by their fine work in the early twentieth century, paved the way for a long overdue return to simplicity and the half-forgotten art of building dignified, pleasant, and serviceable homes.

42 William Morris (1834–96)
From the portrait by G. F. Watts

Chapter V

WILLIAM MORRIS AND THE
PRE-RAPHAELITE BROTHERHOOD

WE have devoted this chapter to one of the most courageous, energetic and likeable personalities of late-nineteenth-century England—a man whose life and work had a profound effect on the design and decoration of Everyday Things. His story opens at the Great Exhibition of 1851, already mentioned in our introductory pages. William Morris (42) was seventeen at the time. Who took him to the Exhibition we do not know; his mother perhaps—it could not have been his father, a respectable bill and discount broker in the City, who had died in 1847. But, whoever it was, here was all the promise of a happy Victorian day. The average Englishman who visited the Crystal Palace and looked down its long vistas saw them continued, beyond reality, into the dreamland of a Golden Age that was to continue for ever, with England as the workshop of the world. Mrs. Morris's breast may have swelled with some such feeling, if she it was who took William. But Morris was no average Englishman; and he spoiled the party by sitting down and refusing to go over the Exhibition, which he declared was "wonderfully ugly".

Here was a pretty kettle of fish for a Victorian mother! Boys, and girls for that matter, who do not react normally can be an infernal nuisance. You cannot very well smack a boy of seventeen, no matter how much you may want to, in the entrance hall of a great exhibition; nor is it a place in which one would willingly enter into a debate on the meaning of the word "ugliness". The point for us, however, is that, although it was a very bad beginning to a Victorian day, it was a very good beginning for William's life work. Morris was to be insurgent as well as artist, and became the leader of a group of men who were to protest against all that the Great Exhibition stood for. There were amazing curiosities there to satisfy the populace; but the real god in the shrine was the machine. Times had been troublous in England; 1848 was the year of widespread revolutions, and we had our own Chartists. So, if the Exhibition was hateful to one group, it was very hopeful to many others. The pity is, of course, that the two groups did not combine.

When we first dealt with the Great Exhibition and its exhibits in Vol. III, we tried to show how it was that people became so strangely insensitive to beauty in their scramble for wealth. Fig. 6 gives just one more reminder of the kind of things that were exhibited in 1851; and it may be that William saw this out of the tail of his eye, and so refused to be taken around. And this strange blight of ugliness was over everything. Architecture, the mother of the arts, was at its lowest ebb. All the gaiety of the Regency period had disappeared, and the monotony of Pimlico and Kensington had taken its place.

Morris was at Marlborough between 1848 and 1851—in those days a very different place from the modern public school. There were no organised games; so Morris employed his leisure in rambles through the country to study old churches and earthworks on the Downs. Even as a schoolboy he was developing his love of Gothic architecture. Having left school, he was sent to Oxford, and sat for the entrance examination in the Hall of Exeter. This was a very important occasion; the boy who sat next to him was Edward Burne-Jones (43), the son and only child of a carver, gilder, and picture-framer in Birmingham. The two boys became fast friends—Burne-Jones was a year older than Morris; and the friendship then established was to endure throughout their lives. Carving, gilding and framing seems a more likely background for an artist than discounting and bill broking. But neither of the youths was intended for an artistic career; both were destined for the Church.

Morris went up to Oxford in 1853; and his work there seems to have left him an ample leisure for study on his own lines. Ruskin's *Seven Lamps of Architecture* had been published in 1849; the first part of his *Stones of Venice* appeared in 1851, and Parts II and III in 1853. In Part II, the sixth chapter was concerned with the "Nature of Gothic"; and this chapter can be taken as one of the formative influences of Morris's life. He always acknowledged it as such; and when later on, towards the end of his life, he set up his own Kelmscott Press, the *Nature of Gothic* was among the first texts that he published. Ruskin

43 "Topsy" [William Morris] and "Ted Jones" [Edward Burne-Jones] on the settle in Red Lion Square

From the watercolour by Max Beerbohm

had been born in 1819, the son of a prosperous wine merchant, who travelled around England on business and took his boy with him. Ruskin went up to Christ Church, Oxford, when he was eighteen. His *Modern Painters* influenced Burne-Jones in much the same way as the *Nature of Gothic* did Morris. But his influence on Morris was particularly deep. It stirred the poetic side of the young man's nature, which afterwards sent him off on his adventurous viking cruise to Iceland.

During our own youth, we happened to catch sight of Morris who was then an old man; and he reminded us of one of the sea rovers of whom we had read in the *Burnt Njal Saga*. When as a young man he opened Ruskin's *Nature of Gothic*, in which the writer suggests that "there will be found something more than usually interesting in tracing out this grey, shadowy many-pinnacled image of the Gothic spirit within us and discerning what fellowship there is between it and our Northern hearts," Morris was profoundly moved. It is said that you must be either Greek or Goth; and by temperament Morris was a Goth.

Another epoch-making moment in his life occurred in 1855, when he and Burne-Jones went to France with a friend named Fulford. The glories of French Gothic were too much for our heroes; they went to France destined for the Church—they returned determined to be artists. Burne-Jones was to paint, and Morris to be an architect. So on 21st January, 1856, we find him entering the office of George Edmund Street, the architect to the Diocese of Oxford, who was then practising in that city. There he met Philip Webb, who was Street's head assistant, and was also to become a lifelong friend. Webb, born 1831, was the son of an Oxford doctor. There is something very moving about the friendship of these three men. They came together when they were young, which is the proper time to make friends; they were all to achieve distinction; yet none of them outgrew the others. They were constantly meeting and talking and laughing and indulging in uproarious practical jokes. Each of them had an appropriate nickname. Burne-Jones was "Ted", and Morris, because of his unruly shock of hair, "Topsy". The world went very well in those days for this Oxford brotherhood.

The friends do not seem to have been very much affected by the troubles of the times. Street moved his office to London in the autumn of 1856, and Morris went with him, but gave up architecture at the end of the year. Burne-Jones had already gone to London and was studying painting under the guidance of Rossetti, who introduced him to Madox-Brown and Holman Hunt. Holman Hunt's "Light of the World" had been exhibited at the Royal Academy in 1854; but the pre-Raphaelite artists did not have it all their own way; and among rival pictures exhibited were a group of the Royal Family in Highland costume and Maclise's "Marriage of Strongbow and Eva". Holman Hunt's "Scapegoat" and Frith's "Derby Day" were both shown at the Royal Academy of 1856. Burne-Jones had got into touch with Rossetti through the Working Men's College, in Great Ormond Street, London, founded by Denison Maurice, where University men lectured on science and history, and Rossetti taught the students drawing.

Morris, too, now fell under the influence of Rossetti, a very dominant personality, and he himself began painting. In 1857, he and Burne-Jones moved to the first floor of 17 Red Lion Square, Holborn, London; and if any of our readers care to visit the house they can see the centre window which gave additional light to the friends' studio. It was the problem of furnishing of these rooms that launched Morris on his life's work. Remember that there was, at that time, practically nothing to be bought ready-made that Burne-Jones or Morris would have cared to live with. This does not mean that the ordinary furniture of the period was shoddy machine-made stuff. On the contrary, it was well made by hand, but uniformly hideous. Strangely enough, antique furniture had not yet come into its own, and was regarded as merely old-fashioned. The Madox-Brown family got over one difficulty by using on their table the common English willow-pattern plates at that time generally relegated to the kitchen. True, Pugin had exhibited furniture; but it was too ecclesiastical for domestic use and too much in the taste of the Gothic Revival. This is a point to be noted here. Although Morris was Goth rather than Greek, he was not by any means a medievalist, a revivalist or a restorer—he wished to carry on and extend the Gothic tradition, adapting it to the needs of modern society.

But now came an important change in William Morris's personal life. In 1857, he fell in love with the lovely and romantic

44 Desk designed by Philip Webb for Morris and Co.

Jane Burden; and, having married her in 1859, he set up house at 41 Great Ormond Street. But this was regarded as only a temporary measure; and the friends started hunting for a site on which a home could be built that was worthy of so beautiful a bride. It was eventually found at Upton, Bexley, Kent; and Webb left Street's office, where he was succeeded by Norman Shaw, in order to design the building. The house, that Webb designed and Morris built, proved to be of the greatest interest; and Webb's admirers like to refer to it as the very first of the Red Houses, which afterwards were to become a common, almost too common, feature of the English countryside. We are not quite sure ourselves that it should be hailed as the very beginning of the school; for George Devey, whose work we mentioned in Chapter IV, was already active. Devey's work, however, was less influential than that of Webb; for Webb designed in collaboration with men like Morris, Burne-Jones and Rossetti. The pre-Raphaelites had the great advantage of working as a united group.

From their endeavours at Red Lion Square and Bexley sprang the firm of Morris, Marshall, Faulkner & Co. Marshall was a friend of Madox-Brown's. Faulkner, an old Oxford friend, then a civil engineer in London, looked after the business side and was a general handyman. Burne-Jones and Madox-Brown made designs for stained glass. Webb designed furniture, and Powell's of Whitefrairs blew glass from his designs. Albert Moore and William de Morgan helped on occasions; and so did Rossetti. When Morris wallpapers were first produced, they were printed by Messrs. Jeffreys. Premises were taken in 1861 at 8 Red Lion Square; and the associates styled themselves "Fine Art *Workmen* in Painting, Carving, Furniture, and the Metals".

96

It is essential to bear in mind that Morris and his associates went into business like good tradesmen. There was nothing dilettante about their efforts; and, as sound workmen and efficient businessmen, they determined to produce attractive objects at a reasonable price. At the outset, much of their combined energy was devoted to the decoration of churches; but they were always deeply interested in beautifying domestic life; and their motto seems to have been: "Have nothing in your houses that you do not know to be useful or believe to be beautiful." As the years passed, Morris's business grew; and by 1865 he had become so busy that he was obliged to give up the Red House, where he had spent what was probably the happiest period of his whole existence. Leaving his Bexley home, with its garden and bowling green, he transported himself and his family to rooms over his shop at 26 Queen Square, Bloomsbury, the Red Lion Square workshops being given up. He was now beginning to burn the candle at both ends. In 1867 the firm decorated the Green Dining-room at the Victoria and Albert Museum at South Kensington; and the good condition in which it remains today testifies to its honest workmanship.

About this time the group strengthened itself by collecting recruits. One of Lady Burne-Jones's sisters married John Lockwood Kipling and had a son, called Rudyard; while another sister married Alfred Baldwin, from whom Stanley Baldwin was descended. Morris, meanwhile, had become sufficiently prosperous to acquire a country house; and in 1871 he bought the Manor House at Kelmscott, near Lechlade, which he shared with Rossetti. This lovely old house was to be a great solace to the friends. Here Morris was able to retire when the business became too much for him and go fishing in the river nearby. Kelmscott was to remain his abiding love; and his other houses, and last of all his press, were named after it. In 1873 he left Queen Square and made his London headquarters in Hammersmith; but once more the business seems to have continually encroached on his living space, until he had to go.

He was always the most active and restless of men; and in 1874 he embarked on a new venture. Experiments were being made with dyes. The old vegetable dyes, indigo, woad, madder, and weld for yellow, had been forgotten, and aniline dyes had taken their place. So Morris plunged into the dye vats. Here he showed his wisdom, by enlisting the help of Thomas Wardle of Leek, a well-known dyer; he seems never to have begun designing until he had mastered the practical details of a craft. At this period Morris often startled his friends by appearing with hands and arms stained blue to the elbow after dabbling in indigo. The first yarns he dyed were apparently used for carpets. Some of the old partners seceded about this time, and the firm became Morris & Co. in 1875.

Now we have reached an especially interesting stage in Morris's career, which marks his first introduction to public life, and shows how far he had advanced ahead of his own time. Terrible outrages were then being perpetrated under the name of "Restoration"; and these artistic crimes were usually committed by clergymen and professional architects. The parsons, particularly if they were zealous priests, wished their churches to look as Gothic as possible; and they were apt to call in the architects, whom they commissioned to restore the building to what they imagined had been its appearance before the Reformation. Perfectly genuine Renaissance work was thrown out and mock "Gothic" stuff put in its place, all manufactured and freshly varnished by church furnishing firms. The classic case of so-called restoration occurred when Butterfield, as a leading Gothicist and the architect of Keble College, Oxford, was commissioned, early in the 'seventies, to restore Winchester College Chapel. Wren had worked there about 1684; and it must have been then that he introduced a very lovely oak screen, wall panelling, and altar rails. The screen had perforated panels, in the manner of the staircase at Guildford we illustrated in Vol. II. "Manners makyth man"; but neither the college authorities nor Butterfield had any architectural manners; and Wren's panelling was ripped out and sold for an old song. It was not "Gothic"—that was excuse enough.

It was around the year 1877, when Sir Gilbert Scott was contemplating an onslaught on Tewkesbury Abbey, that Morris rushed into the fray. He wrote to the *Athenaeum*, suggesting that old buildings were of undoubted historical value; that when, in the thirteenth century, men wished to alter or add to a Norman building, they did not do it in sham Norman, but in the workmanship of their own period; and so the process had gone on throughout the ages, with the result that the ancient structure could nowadays be read almost as we read a document. To attempt to "restore" a building was to attempt the impossible —he pleaded for reparation, so that the fabric should be preserved, rather than for restoration, which destroyed its genuine character. This led to the formation of the Society for the Protection of Ancient Buildings in 1877; and Morris was its first secretary. Carlyle was a supporter of what became known as the "Anti-Scrape" movement; and but for the work which it did then, and has done since, there would hardly be an old building, recognisable as such, left to us in the twentieth century.

So far as Morris's own work was concerned, dyeing, calico printing and weaving were now much to the fore; and a new show-room was opened in Oxford Street, opposite the present site of Selfridge's. In 1878 he added lecturing on the Decorative Arts to his other activities and took a house in the Upper Mall, Hammersmith, where he passed the remainder of his life, altering its name to Kelmscott House, as a tribute to his beloved home in the country. Here he had a tapestry loom put up in his bedroom, so that he could work at it if he happened to wake at an early hour. This was typical of the man—he had decided to revive the art of high-warp tapestry weaving; and having looked ahead and foreseen that, with Burne-Jones's help, fine work could be done, he began to experiment himself until he understood the medium. It is interesting to note that he has gone back to a type of which we described the origins in our volume on *Homeric Greece*. In that book Penelope is depicted weaving the shroud for Laertes on a high-warp loom. Carpet looms were installed in the converted stables of Morris's house from which came the beautiful Hammersmith carpets. 1878, however, was a bad year in the annals of the brotherhood; Morris, who, as usual, had been overworking, contracted rheumatic gout, and the group as a whole received a serious challenge.

Pre-Raphaelitism had at length expended its strength; and a new artistic school was knocking at the door. In 1878 the *Whistler* v. *Ruskin* action was heard in the Law Courts—a fight between two schools rather than a clash between two men. It came about because James McNeill Whistler (1834–1903) objected to Ruskin's unkind criticism of his pictures at the newly founded Grosvenor Gallery, which, he asserted, was highly damaging to his artistic reputation. A mettlesome and

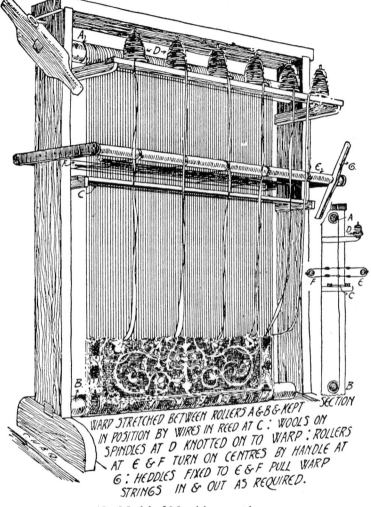

WARP STRETCHED BETWEEN ROLLERS A & B & KEPT
IN POSITION BY WIRES IN REED AT C : WOOLS ON
SPINDLES AT D KNOTTED ON TO WARP : ROLLERS
AT E & F TURN ON CENTRES BY HANDLE AT
G : HEDDLES FIXED TO E & F PULL WARP
STRINGS IN & OUT AS REQUIRED.

45   Model of Morris's carpet loom
Victoria and Albert Museum

oellicose individual, he struck back at Ruskin as the pre-
Raphaelite High Priest. The action turned on good craftsmanship. Burne-Jones gave evidence on Ruskin's behalf, and said
that he thought perfect finish was necessary. In his judgment
"The Nocturne in Blue and Silver" was "an incomplete work

of art", and "Battersea Bridge" was "formless". "The Nocturne in Black and Gold" he did not think could be ranked as a work of art at all. A Titian was produced in court as an illustration of finish. The lawyers thoroughly enjoyed themselves, and in the end Whistler got a farthing damages without costs. But the pre-Raphaelite School, and all that it stood for, had sustained a heavy blow. As the "Nocturne in Blue and Silver", the "Nocturne in Black and Gold", and the "Symphony in White, No 2", are now at the National Gallery, and "Old Battersea Bridge" and two fine portraits at the Tate, our readers can pay them a visit and, while doing so, may form their own judgment.

In 1881 Morris & Co. moved to Merton Abbey, where his tapestry-making really got under way. The technical difficulties of reviving this ancient craft must have been enormous. Then, in 1882, he cast in his lot with the Socialists. Here he was deeply influenced by Ruskin's *Unto this Last*, which first appeared as a series of articles in the *Cornhill Magazine*, and was published in book form in 1862. Read today, it seems the mildest reminder that working for profit is not the final end and aim of existence. But, at the time, it appeared to be a dangerous revolutionary work—aimed at the foundations of the Victorian economic system, which authorised the employer to regulate wages according to the law of supply and demand, extorting the maximum amount of labour for the smallest sum that the labourer could be persuaded to accept. Ruskin denounced this principle, and even went so far as to suggest that an employer should learn to respect and love the human beings whom he employed!

With his customary drive and enthusiasm, Morris threw himself into the Socialist cause, and preached at street corners and addressed meetings all over England. But Burne-Jones could not follow him; it was the one interest that they did not share. Morris would go to breakfast on Sunday mornings with Burne-Jones, and then leave to do his Socialist work and preach the Gospel as he interpreted it. He was dominated by Socialism until about 1886, when, although he still worked hard in the cause, he turned back to his own creative endeavours. In 1888, through his friendship with Emery Walker, he became interested in typography; and this led to the foundation of the Kelmscott Press. Typography, or the art of the printed page, was then at a very low ebb, except for the work of a few men like Walker, who were doing their best to improve the standard. Morris wanted to turn out gloriously decorated books; and in this he was helped by Walker, who, without becoming a business partner, gave advice as a friend, while Burne-Jones provided many of the decorations. In 1890 the new Kelmscott type was being designed. Producing good type is a matter of the greatest difficulty. The first essential is that it should be clear to read and good to look at. Printing was begun in 1891; and the first book that Morris published was *The Story of the Glittering Plain*. In 1892 came Ruskin's *On the Nature of Gothic*, extracted from the *Stones of Venice*; and in his Preface Morris explained the effect that this book had had upon his life and work. The great Kelmscott *Chaucer* was his last work; he died on October 3rd, 1896, aged sixty-three, worn out by having attempted to do the work of seven men; and with the death of William Morris an epoch closed.

Professor Mackail, in his *Life*, has published a delightful letter from Morris to Webb dated August 27th, 1894. Morris had been sending Webb the Kelmscott Press books as they appeared, and Webb had evidently remonstrated with him at the extent of his generosity. So in his letter, which begins "My dear Fellow" and ends "Yours affectionately", Morris tells the tale of a traveller in the United States who entered an inn and ordered chicken for his dinner. The clerk who received the order answered by taking out a revolver and, after covering the guest, remarked, "Stranger, you will not have chicken, you will have hash"—Webb, in short, was to have the Kelmscott books as they came out, whether he liked it or not.

There can be no doubt that it was the astounding vigour of Morris that animated the pre-Raphaelite group. After his death, the Arts and Crafts Movement faded out of the picture, to have a renaissance a little later on the Continent. People were no longer interested in "tracing out this grey, shadowy, many-pinnacled image of the Gothic spirit within us and discerning what fellowship there is between it and our Northern hearts"; Beowulf and Arthur and the heroes of the *Burnt Njal Saga* retired into the shadows, and English readers turned back to the modern world. Burne-Jones died in 1898, while Webb, apparently disheartened, retired in 1900. But the pre-Raphaelite Brotherhood had left its mark on English history.

Chapter VI

HOUSEHOLD MANAGEMENT AND FURNISHING

WE must now return to the workaday world, to ordinary men and women, and their humdrum, but absorbing, daily lives. The Victorian housewife was usually an excellent manager; and the house that she managed was an extremely orderly and well-run place. Young girls were carefully trained in household management before they married. In simple families, where there was only one servant, the daughters gained valuable experience by doing a good deal of cooking and housework themselves. In wealthier homes this was not necessary; but here too the girls were taught the arts of catering, carving and stillroom work, and all the duties of a hostess and housewife. Women in those days did not take much interest in outside affairs; but in their own homes they were supreme; and every husband expected even a young bride to know how to run his house smoothly and well.

Servants' wages were then very low, and almost everyone could afford to employ at least one maid. In middle-class households there were usually two or three, and in larger houses many more, as well as menservants. This made the work lighter for the individual; but there was always a great deal to be done. Labour-saving devices were practically unknown, and houses were not designed to make the daily round easier. Much time was taken up in carrying coal and food upstairs; stone-paved halls and long passages, kitchens, sculleries and front-door steps needed continual scrubbing. The heavy furniture, often elaborately carved (46), required constant polishing, and two or three substantial meals had to be prepared and served every day.

Work began in the kitchen (50) about six o'clock in the morning and went on until the last dishes were washed and put away at night. Early rising was an almost universal rule, especially for the servants, who had to clean the dining-room and the hall, carry hot water up to the bedrooms, and serve a

103

cooked breakfast by eight o'clock. In many households family prayers were held before the meal; and to this all the maids went, kneeling in their rustling, starched print dresses at one end of the room, while the head of the house read morning prayers and passages from the Bible. Every member of the family was expected to appear in the dining-room, for breakfast in bed was not encouraged, except in cases of illness or on rare occasions like the morning after a ball. Rigid punctuality was insisted upon at this and every other meal, so that the servants might not be hindered in clearing away by the presence of late-comers.

The kitchen, though underground and generally lit by artificial light, was a warm and cheerful room (50), furnished with deal

46 A dining-room sideboard of "Queen Anne" type, 1881

By R. W. Edis

104

47 A late-Victorian dolls' house, with attic artist's studio
In the Victoria and Albert Museum

48, 49   Nursery and kitchen to larger scale

50 · A Victorian kitchen, 1869
By John Leech

tables and a dresser, chairs for meals, and perhaps a couple of Windsor armchairs for leisure moments. A huge range fitted with ovens and boilers consumed enormous quantities of coal, which was then much cheaper than it is now. Batteries of iron or copper saucepans reflected its flames, and with them hung frying-pans, skillets, skimmers and sieves of varying fineness. A good cook expected to be supplied with numerous fancy moulds for puddings, jellies and aspic dishes, as well as preserving pans, bread tins, milk bowls, and other utensils.

Bread was always baked at home in the country and quite often in the towns, and all cakes were made there. A vast amount of bottling, preserving, jam-making and pickling went on every summer; and some women also made their own fruit wines and cordials. A well-stocked store-cupboard was the housewife's pride, and practically all its contents were prepared by herself and her maids. Canned foods, such as we constantly buy now, were not included. They were known, it is true, and were frequently used by sailors on long voyages, or by travellers in remote places. But the art of canning was then in its infancy, and tinned goods were still viewed with a certain amount of suspicion by the careful caterer.

106

In the scullery or, if there was one, the wash-house, coppers and wooden tubs stood ready for the family laundry, which was nearly always done at home. This was a considerable undertaking, for the elaborate fashions of the time necessitated much starching, pleating and gophering of frilly petticoats, and the careful treatment of fine laces and organdie. Some housewives washed once a week, as we do, but others preferred to have one huge washing-day at intervals of a month or six weeks. This suggests that everybody must have had a good supply of linen to last out so long; and, in fact, they usually had. Underclothes were made in six or twelve complete sets at a time, usually of good strong longcloth or cambric which did not wear out quickly; and linen-cupboards were normally well stocked with all the sheets, towels, pillow-cases and other requirements of a large family.

A mixture of comfort and discomfort, of hard work and leisure, was the keynote of most homes at this period. The Victorians, in spite of their love of display, had a Spartan strain in their characters that enabled them to put up with, and indeed not notice, the lack of many little comforts that nowadays we take for granted. As a rule, they were well and generously fed; and this perhaps helped them to ignore the fact that their houses were often very cold in winter, especially in the passages where the absence of central heating or hall-stoves gave full play to the draughts. Good fires were usual in the sitting-rooms and kitchens; but there was little warmth elsewhere,

51 The hip bath

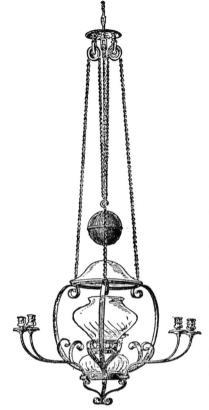

52   A hanging lamp for mineral oil and candles, 1881

and in many families fires in bedrooms were considered an unnecessary luxury except in times of sickness, or when a hip bath was being taken there(51).

Oil lamps were still widely used for illumination, especially in the country(52). These gave a soft, clear light which was very restful to the eyes; but they involved a good deal of work in filling and cleaning. In the towns, gas lamps were more fashionable, either in the form of wall-brackets or of large cast-iron or brass gaseliers which hung from the centre of the ceiling. The flames were protected by glass shades, at first quite plain, like oil-lamp chimneys, and later on shaped like globes, coloured pink or amber, and sometimes decorated with floral designs. As a rule, however, gas lamps were restricted to the main sitting-rooms, hall and kitchen. The rest of the house, including the bedrooms, were lit by lamps or simply by candles. A row of candlesticks was placed every night on the hall table; and as each person retired, he took one upstairs with him, and by its small light undressed and went to bed.

Bathrooms, with hot water laid on, were not common until the end of the nineteenth century. "No house of any pretensions will be devoid of a general Bathroom,"[1] wrote the architect Robert Kerr, in 1865; but, in fact, a good many fair-sized houses were devoid of these conveniences in his day. This was not

[1] Robert Kerr, *The English Gentleman's House*, 1865.

108

always due to lack of money or enterprise on the part of the householder. To many Victorians the notion of a single communal bath, which all used in turn, was faintly disgusting. Where a bathroom existed, it was usually an ordinary small room converted for the purpose, containing a fireplace, a wood-rimmed metal bath, and sometimes a shower-bath (53). The water was heated by the kitchen fire. Towards the end of the century, a fitted bathroom became much more usual, though even then it was not thought necessary to include one in designs for cottages and small dwellings, and even large houses rarely had more than one. But at the beginning of our period the most ordinary method of bathing was in a hip bath with a high back (51), or in a flat shallow pan of metal painted to look like wood.

This was kept, when not in use, in the housemaid's closet, or under the bed. When wanted, it was set before the fire, with large towels spread under it to protect the carpet from splashes. It was filled with hot water brought up from the basement in metal cans, and in it the bather sat soaking and warming himself in comfort, without having to worry about keeping others waiting

53   A family bathroom party, 1861
By John Leech

109

if he dallied too long. A screen, or covered towel-horse, behind protected him from draughts; and, when he was ready to get out, there were towels already warming before the fire in which to wrap himself.

It was in their sitting-rooms that the Victorians mainly indulged their love of colour and complicated detail, and their desire for massive and imposing furniture. A rich and splendid comfort was the well-to-do householder's ambition; and to achieve this he bought large mahogany tables and sideboards (46), with chairs to match, for his dining-room, and armchairs and sofas covered with damask or striped silk, and a variety of little tables and cabinets, for his drawing-room. Long curtains of velvet, serge or damask hung at the windows; patterned carpets, of intricate design and very decided hue, covered the floors. Occasional tables, reading-stands, embroidered footstools and carved bookcases stood about in profusion; and there was nearly always a grand or upright piano in the drawing-room, a bureau for writing, and a rosewood needlework table.

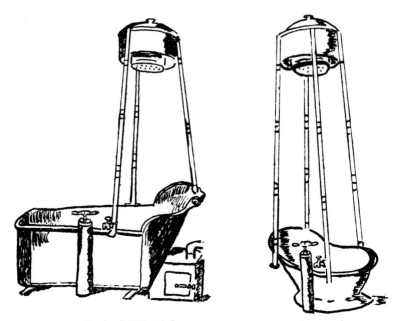

54   Baths (1855–60) from a contemporary catalogue of
George Jennings (Lambeth)

55 "Modern Gothic" washstand, 1896

The general effect was rather too overcrowded for beauty and, indeed, some rooms seem at first sight to be crammed almost to bursting point. A nervous or clumsy person must often have found it difficult to steer his way without knocking something over, and it is perhaps not surprising that the art of graceful walking was still included in the education of most young ladies.

Knick-knacks of every kind abounded. In the corner-cupboards were displays of china. On small tables, or on the mantelpiece, there were ornamental vases, candlesticks, and wax flowers under glass domes. Numerous pictures in gilded frames hung on the walls, and there were always a good many embroidered cushions, runners, mats, bell-ropes, firescreens, and antimacassars worked by the daughters of the house.

The wallpapers, like the carpets, were heavily patterned in damask or floral designs. Dark reds, greens and blues were the favourite colours, and these were repeated in the long, thick curtains. Deep shades and deep-toned woods might have made Victorian rooms unbearably dark, had it not recently become possible to provide them with larger and more numerous windows. The window tax was abolished in 1851, so that there

111

was no longer any economic reason for restricting the number of windows, and the introduction of plate-glass allowed the use of larger single panes, which admitted much more light than the old small sections. A direct result of this improvement was the almost universal fashion for white Nottingham lace curtains. These hung between the windows and the heavier serge or damask curtains, and were intended both to screen the room from prying eyes in the street and to diffuse the light. Both these things they did with great efficiency.

In the bedrooms, enormous oak and mahogany wardrobes and large beds took up much of the space. Four-poster beds, with side-curtains that could be drawn at night, were still usual at the beginning of our period. Later on, they were replaced by iron or brass bedsteads, which were probably healthier but were decidedly less attractive. There was a good deal of frilliness in most of these rooms. Frilled valances ran round the bottom of

56 Mahogany high chair, seat covered with horsehair, about 1860
Bethnal Green Museum, London

the bed; starched and frilled muslin, lined with coloured silk, draped the dressing-table and its mirror. In one corner stood a marble-topped washstand, with a jug and basin of plain or patterned china (55). Flowers, particularly roses and violets, appeared in the wallpaper and the carpet; and sometimes there were chintz curtains similarly patterned at the windows.

The servants slept in the attics, which also included box-rooms. Two rooms were generally set aside as nurseries; and one as a schoolroom where the older children were taught by their governess. These were apt to be rather sparsely furnished places, comfortable enough, but unadorned. Plain chairs and tables, serge tablecloths and simple rag rugs, were thought quite good enough for children's destructive little hands and feet.

While most people were cramming their rooms with up-holstered chairs and sofas, with deep-piled carpets and thick draught-proof curtains, William Morris (as we explained in Chapter V) was preaching a more austere style (57, 58). In his own house he had straight-backed armchairs softened only by loose cushions, and smaller chairs with plaited rush or osier seats. Instead of polished mahogany, he used plain woods that could be scrubbed for his tables, and set them at meal-times with glass specially blown to his own designs and blue-and-white willow-patterned china. Eastern rugs lay here and there on the floors; the fireplaces were of ex-posed brick, unadorn-ed by the elaborate overmantels then fashionable, and the stairs were of simple, uncarpeted oak (59).

Most people were not prepared to go so far, however much they admired medie-val styles in theory. But in this, as in so much else, Morris's influence was strong enough to effect a definite change in fashion, even though the results were often far removed from the austere simplicity of his original ideas. In the last twenty years of the nine-teenth century, Morris

57 Hall settle, the Red House, Bexley
Philip Webb, Architect, 1859

113

furniture, or imitations of it, and Morris wallpapers became the rage. Householders abandoned the harsh, bright pinks, crimsons and magentas of earlier years and bought curtains and carpets in soft blues and greys, dull olive-greens, and creamy whites or yellows. Hand-woven fabrics, hand-made china and pottery, hammered metal-work, and peacocks' feathers appeared in every drawing-room; and there was also a craze for Japanese fans and screens, and for light bamboo furniture, which sometimes sat rather oddly among the heavier mahogany and rosewood pieces left over from the previous fashion.

Much really lovely work. was done at this time by artist-craftsmen like Ernest Gimson, or Sidney and Ernest Barnsley. These three men were architects who, like Morris, were deeply impressed by the beauty of old handicrafts. Their interests extended beyond the building of houses to the making of furniture; and, as they were themselves skilled craftsmen, they were able to work out their own ideas in metal, wood and stone.

They founded a workshop in the Cotswolds; and here, in addition to building cottages of local stone, and encouraging local smiths to produce fine wrought-iron work, they designed and made beautiful chairs, tables (61), cabinets, and many other articles for the home.

Their furniture preserved the best traditions of old English workmanship; but it was no mere imitation of ancient styles. Each piece was made from the maker's own design, and intended

58   Dining-room sideboard, the Red House
Philip Webb, Architect, 1859

by him for daily use, so that it was comfortable and serviceable, as well as pleasing to the eye. Little carving was employed in decoration, but there was much fine inlay work. The natural colours and markings of the wood were left showing, without the addition of dark stains or polishes. This in itself was something new at that time, for deep-toned woods had been fashionable for years. Almost all mid-Victorian furniture was dark and highly polished. But in the Cotswold pieces the actual hues and marks of walnut, oak or mahogany were allowed to contribute their full share to the total effect, just as in former ages the glowing colours and grain of unstained woods had contributed to the brightness of medieval solars and Elizabethan long galleries.

The work of Gimson and the Barnsleys was necessarily expensive; for much time and skill were involved, and in their small workshop they could not hope to produce any really large quantity of goods. Only the well-to-do could afford to buy their furniture, and to many it remained practically unknown. But from about 1897 onwards the tradition of fine but simple designs was carried into the

59   The staircase, the Red House
Philip Webb, Architect

115

homes of ordinary people by Sir Ambrose Heal (62). Being a manufacturer and not a handicraftsman, he could produce more cheaply and in far larger quantities than the Cotswold designers, and by so doing he did much to educate the public taste.

The deep interest in the remote past shown by Morris and his followers also turned people's thoughts towards antique furniture of more recent date. In the mid-Victorian years many lovely old Georgian and Stuart pieces had been sold, or pushed into the attics to make room for newer belongings. Now they were brought out again and their fine proportions viewed with a new and more appreciative eye. Collecting antique furniture became a hobby for the rich; and those who could not afford to buy genuine old stuff contented themselves with imitation or faked goods which were at least sufficiently like the real thing to satisfy the uncritical.

This renewed appreciation of good former styles was not, however, altogether due to Morris's influence. Much of it was caused by the reaction against a hideous fashion of the late nineties which was known as the "New Art" (*L'Art Nouveau*). This fortunately short-lived craze was certainly new, but only by the widest stretch of the imagination could it be described as Art. It spread to England from the Continent and flooded English homes with curves and arabesques, with carved scrolls and twisted ornaments, and flimsy, over-decorated furniture (63). Everything was covered with wriggling patterns of stems and leaves, with painted flowers or stencilled traceries of loops and curling lines. A plain surface, if by chance it could be

60   6-inch De Morgan tile

found, became as precious as an open space in a jungle. Whatever underlying design there may have been was lost in the too-luxuriant profusion of detail, and the total effect was extremely restless. After a few years people turned with relief from this pretentious and insincere style to the pleasantly tranquil lines of eighteenth-century furniture.

During the Edwardian period, which began in 1901, household work and management became easier in many different ways. Fitted bathrooms were by now quite common, so that there was much less carrying of water to be done. Basement kitchens were no longer included in newly built houses, which meant less running up and down stairs, hotter food in the dining-room, and fewer front-door steps to scrub. It meant, too, that servants had more light and air than was possible in an underground room; and when they looked out of the windows they could see something more interesting than the boots of passers-by moving above their heads. The vast coal-eating ranges of former years were being replaced by the cleaner and more convenient gas stove; and oil lamps disappeared and gave place to gas or electric light (11) in almost every room.

The first electric lamps were not very effective, and most people still preferred the clear light of gas lamps, which had been greatly improved by the introduction of incandescent mantles. A favourite form of lighting at this period was by a type of gaselier that hung from the centre of the ceiling. It had two or three lamps on it, attached to a movable arm which could be turned in any direction so as to bring the light wherever it was most wanted. Usually there was a large circular shade of rose-coloured or golden silk, the material of which was fluted and trimmed with ruching or fringe round the edges. Wall-brackets with coloured

61   Table in English oak, about 1910
By E. W. Gimson

silk shades were also common; but bedside and reading-desk lamps had to wait until the use of electricity became more general. So, too, did wall switches. Old-fashioned gaseliers were lit by matches; the more up-to-date had a small pilot flame known as the bypass which glowed continuously at the bottom of the lamp and lit it when a chain attached to a small metal bar was pulled.

After a time, the early electric carbon bulbs were replaced by more powerful bulbs with metallic filaments. Another innovation that was to have far-reaching effects was the telephone. This American invention was first used in England in the late nineteenth century. London had telephones as early as the 'seventies(2); but they were chiefly confined to business houses, whence they slowly spread to private dwellings. The instrument itself was fixed to the wall, usually in the hall or in a passage; and the user stood with his mouth close to the fixed mouthpiece and, after turning a handle to establish communication with the exchange, said what he had to say in full hearing of any member of the household who might be within earshot. It was not a comfortable way of doing things, but no one thought of indulging in the long aimless telephone conversations that are so popular today.

Edwardian rooms, like the houses that contained them, were much lighter and gayer than those of the Victorian period. There was less heavy furniture, and more room to move about; colours were more delicate, and real flowers were more freely used in decoration. In the drawing-room comfortable armchairs were shrouded in loose, washable covers of printed chintz or

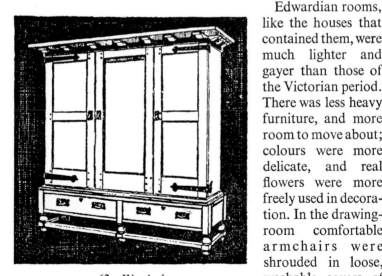

62 Wardrobe
By Ambrose Heal, 1897

118

cretonne, with pleasant flower designs in natural shades. Wall-papers were light and fresh, and carpets far less heavily pat-terned than formerly. In some houses, cane furniture was used. This was a fashion introduced by B. J. Fletcher, Principal of the Leicester School of Art. While on holiday in Austria, he had seen examples of this work and was so pleased with it that he brought a cane chair home with him and taught his art students how to make others. In 1907, the "Dryad" Cane Furniture Works was founded, and from that date onwards this light and durable form of furniture (64) became very popular.

In the bedrooms, wooden bedsteads were beginning to replace the hideous brass or iron erections of the late nineteenth century. Muslin or dimity cur-tains were often used, and gave a pleasantly fresh effect; and white- or green-painted furni-ture was not unusual, especially in rooms occu-pied by children or young girls.

The piano was still as highly prized a posses-sion as in Victorian times (11); for people still made their own music at home. A grand piano of polished rosewood or dully gleaming ebony, its flat top covered with photographs in silver frames and vases of flowers, was every house-wife's ambition. If she could not achieve it, she had a small up-right piano, backed by fluted silk in pink or yellow. Very often there was another in the

63 Cabinet in the *Art Nouveau* style, about 1900

Bethnal Green Museum, London

64 The "Dryad" wicker chair, 1908

school-room on which the children practised. In most middle-class households, children were taught music as a matter of course, without any regard to their particular talents or wishes.

The nearest approach to mechanical music was the phonograph, which was followed, early in the twentieth century, by the gramophone. The former was a portable machine with a large horn for sound-transmission shaped like a huge convolvulus flower. The music was recorded on cylinders of chocolate-coloured wax, which were placed on a revolving roller; and the whole machine was wound up like a clockwork toy. Neither the phonograph nor the gramophone, in its early stages, was a very good instrument. But both gave a great deal of pleasure in their day. As a means of enjoying music at home, however, or as an accompaniment to dancing, the piano reigned supreme throughout the Edwardian era; and there were few houses of any pretensions that did not contain one of these instruments and at least one member of the family who could play it competently and well.

Chapter VII

DRESS AND FASHION

CLOTHES are always interesting to study, not only because they reveal the taste of the wearer and, to some extent, his character, but also because they tell us something about the period in which they were worn. Fashions change constantly; and at first sight they may seem to do so at random, or to have been dictated simply by the whims and fancies of dress designers. Actually, there is a reason for every change. Clothes reflect the thoughts and habits of the time and alter with them; and, if we look carefully at the customary dress of any given period, we can usually learn a good deal about the people's ways, ideas, and general outlook on life.

In a gay and luxurious age, for instance, dresses tend to be elaborate, brightly coloured, and made of rich materials. In a more serious age they will be sober, plain in cut and quiet in tone. Changing ideas of decorum may make what was suitable and becoming in one century appear comic, and even indecent, in another. Our great-grandmothers would have thought it outrageous for a woman to wear slacks, which we think quite normal; but then we would probably consider the ankle-length pantaloons worn by little girls in 1850 decidedly peculiar (65). Again, when class distinctions were clear-cut and rigid, there was a sharp division between the clothes of rich and poor. It was then quite easy to tell a man's social position simply by noticing his style of dress. It would have been considered most unsuitable for a working-man to imitate the fashions of wealthier folk; and, indeed, he had neither the wish nor the means to do so. In our own more democratic days, everyone wears much the same *sort* of clothes, even though materials and cut still vary with the individual income.

Changing notions of health affect fashion; and so do daily habits. It is not so long ago that children were smothered in a multitude of flannel petticoats for their health's sake, just as now, for precisely the same reason, they are encouraged to run free in as few garments as possible. Hoops and crinolines (66, 127,

65   Children's outdoor dress, 1855

139, 140) were popular when women spent most of their time indoors; and men wore smoking-caps and jackets when pipes and cigars were only tolerated in the garden or in a room specially set apart. Smoking-jackets vanished when smoking all over the house was allowed; and short skirts and tailor-made suits came in when women began to lead a more active outdoor life.

At the beginning of our period, as we have seen, the middle classes were coming into power; and it was their ideas that had most influence on the fashions of the time. We see this at once in men's clothes. Ten years earlier, it was still customary for men to wear coloured coats and white or light-hued trousers. In 1844, we read in *Punch* that the correct morning dress for a gentleman was a "blue frock-coat, white drill trousers, and a white stock"; in the evening, long-tailed coloured coats, light trousers, white waistcoats and cravats were worn. In any masculine assembly, a variety of greens, blues, buffs, browns and greys were to be seen, with here and there the gleam of gilt buttons and the glossy sheen of satin cravats. The old love of colour, which had made men's clothes so brilliant in previous centuries, was not yet extinct; and the general effect of masculine attire before 1850 was cheerful, graceful and pleasing.

By 1855, however, we see a great change. Fashions had become darker, more uniform and far less interesting. Sober business men felt that gay hues were not suitable in a hard-working, utilitarian age; and they preferred clothes that were richly plain rather than gaily coloured. Black frock-coats of a simpler cut replaced the blues and greens of the previous decade.

122

66 Blue and white striped dress with lace collar and pleated bodice and skirt.
Belt and sleeve bands of bright blue ribbon with black edge. 1851.
London Museum.

67 A bridesmaid's dress, 1860, of cream silk, flower patterned, with green
ruching and lace flounce. Bodice laced at back and skirt with large double pleats.
London Museum.

68 Olive green cloth dress with brown silk frills, braid and embroidery, and
bow. 1875. *Le Journal des Modes.*

69 An evening dress, 1875, of silver-grey silk with frills and bows of silk.
Trimmed with red roses. *The Milliner and Dressmaker.*

66–9 Ladies' costume, 1851–75

White evening waistcoats were exchanged for black ones; and morning trousers were now made of the checked materials that became so popular after the Great Exhibition.

It was not usual to have coat and trousers of the same stuff; and this at first somewhat relieved the dull effect. But the reign of drabness had begun; and from that time onwards colour and individual fancy largely disappeared from men's dress. There was much less scope for the display of personal tastes than there had been earlier; and where the Georgian dandy could express himself in fine laces and bright fabrics of every shade, the Victorian was thrown back upon a mere coloured cravat or neckerchief, a fancy waistcoat or gold-topped cane, and the new fashion of wearing ornate beards and whiskers.

Charles Dickens tells us in *Bleak House* what a would-be smart young man of not very high standing looked like in 1852. One of the characters in this book wore "an entirely new suit of glossy clothes, a shiny hat, black kid gloves, a neckerchief of a variety of colours, a large hothouse flower in his buttonhole, and a thick gold ring upon his little finger. Besides which he quite scented the dining-room with bear's grease and other perfumery." We are not told how his trousers looked; but probably they were patterned with rather large checks and fitted very tightly to his leg, in a manner designed to show off an elegant figure to advantage. They may even have been strapped under his instep, though this fashion was already dying out by 1852. On a cold day, he would wear a short double-breasted overcoat, which reached to his knee and was fastened right up to his throat with large buttons.

The Victorians liked good heavy materials for their clothes, as they did for their curtains and furniture. Frock-coats were made of excellent broadcloth, with silk or velvet facings on the lapels. Waistcoats of equally good stuff were cut low to show a silk or satin cravat, with a high, starched collar above it, and a gold pin to keep it in place. The well-to-do wore large gold watches and a gold Albert watch-chain; their gloves were of thick kid and were often hand-made. In towns, top hats were generally worn, though they were not always of the glossy type that became fashionable later on. The whole effect was soberly rich and solid, but rather dull and not a little pompous.

124

70   "Swells" or "Mashers", 1861
By John Leech

There were other styles, however, some of which would seem very strange to us now. Loose tweeds were worn in the country all through Queen Victoria's reign, and became very popular towards the end of it. When bicycling came into fashion in the seventies, men wore special bicycling suits, which consisted of a tweed coat, braided trousers, Hessian boots, and a bowler hat with a jaunty feather sticking up on one side. About 1860 the "mashers" or "heavy swells" appeared, to startle their elders by their dashing and unconventional dress(70).

They usually wore trousers patterned with large squares of black and brown, sometimes of "peg-top" design, with the upper part cut very loose. Their coats were short and often highly coloured; their waistcoats were green or yellow checked with black, and adorned with heavy brass buttons. They favoured thick watch-chains and large nosegays in their button-holes; and some sported an eyeglass on a wide black ribbon hung round the neck. Yellow boots, a "pepper-and-salt" over-coat, and a stovepipe hat completed their day dress; and at night they wore cutaway coats and full, swinging opera cloaks. Not everyone who would have liked it could afford to be a "heavy swell", for such extravagances were costly, and in any case the reign of the mashers did not last very long. About 1880 young men began to turn to quieter styles, and flamboyant clothes went out of fashion.

One fashion that added considerably to the rather heavy effect of men's dress in the mid-Victorian period was the wearing of beards and whiskers. In the eighteenth century most men were clean-shaven. Then, at the beginning of the nineteenth, smart young men took to wearing side-whiskers and what a journal of the day described as "an appendage of hair called a mus-tachio"; and to these the full beard was added about 1854. The Crimean War was then being fought, and officers at the front let their beards grow for purely practical reasons. Certainly they had no intention of setting a new fashion; but the result pleased the Victorian eye, and the mode spread rapidly from military men on active service to civilians at home.

A beard gives an effect of age and respectability to most faces; and the Victorian householder, even if he was still young, liked to look solid and dependable. We remember seeing a portrait of our own grandfather when he was only twenty-five and wore a thick black beard and moustache. He looked much older then, and decidedly more solemn than he did when we knew him in his clean-shaven latter years. For a time men's faces were almost hidden by a wealth of hair; for, besides beards and moustaches, many wore long side-whiskers, popularly known as "Piccadilly weepers", or as "Dundreary whiskers", after a character in a play produced in 1858. The vogue of beards did not last very long; but side-whiskers of a luxuriant and flowing type remained in fashion until as late as 1870. After that they gradually diminished in size and magnificence, until eventually the pendulum of taste swung right over, and it became as usual to be clean-shaven as it had been in the eighteenth century.

Nevertheless, despite "heavy swells", and the "toffs" and "knuts" who succeeded them at the end of the nineteenth century and the beginning of the twentieth, men's fashions did

71   Black mantle, bottle-green silk dress with black bands. **Pink roses and black lace on black bonnet**, trimmed with green. 1853. *Le Journal des Modes*.

72   Green dress, black buttons and braid trimming with white undersleeve and lace collar. Black-and-white lace cap with red roses. 1858. *Le Monde-Elégant*.

73   Buff cloth dress with green silk frills and waistcoat of white lace. Green-and-black hat with buff feather. 1870. *The Milliner and Dressmaker*.

74   Brown costume, trimmed with blue silk. Brown hat, blue ribbons and brown feathers. Fur muff. 1871. *The Milliner and Dressmaker*.

75   Buff and brown striped dress, brown satin sleeves, revers, pocket, and under tunic. Brown hat and feather, red flowers, white collar and cuffs, brown satin tie. 1875. *Le Journal des Modes*.

71–5 Ladies' outdoor costume, 1853–75

not really change very much. Top-hats and frock-coats were worn right up to the outbreak of the Great War in 1914, and masculine clothes in general remained dull and sombre-hued. In the eighteenth century men had been as splendid as peacocks, but in the Industrial Age that followed they became as sober as rooks. It was the women who provided all the sartorial colour and variety of the Victorian scene; and it was their clothes that most clearly reflected the moods of the time, as a still pool reflects the floating clouds.

The average Victorian matron lived a secure and untroubled life, protected by her menfolk from all the hard shocks of life, and expected in return to leave all business and public affairs to them. The "ideal woman" of the day was a modest, retiring creature who ruled in her own household but took very little interest in anything outside it. She rarely meddled in politics or legal matters, and she never dreamt of claiming equality with men. She was quite content to be a good housewife and a charming hostess, a devoted mother, and, of course, a loving and obedient wife. Moreover, in spite of the fact that she led an extremely busy life and often had a large family of children, she was always supposed to be a "delicate female" who could not be

76   Operators at work in the Central Telegraph Office, London, 1871

77 Pink organdie dress with white tartan line over black silk. Black silk plastrons on front of dress, black kilting, piping and cuffs. 1879. *Victoria and Albert Museum.*

78 Red velvet dress with turned back white lace. Train and sleeves edged lace; under-dress ruched green silk. 1880. *Le Journal des Modes.*

79 Maroon voile dress with white collar and cuffs. Pleated satin front and buttons. Sixteen yards of material. 1883. *Myra's Journal.*

80 White figured-silk dress with lace overskirt. Tulle chemisette, humming-birds, and pearl trimming. 1885. *Le Journal des Modes.*

81 White muslin dress, trimmed torchon lace. 1885. *Victoria and Albert Museum.*

82 White silk dress with spotted tulle and pleated panels. Red velvet bows and streamers. 1894. *Le Journal des Modes.*

77–82 Ladies' costume, 1879–94

expected to bear much hardship, and would almost certainly faint or swoon if exposed to the smallest shock or emergency.

In fact, of course, the real woman was not nearly as silly or as self-centred as her menfolk liked to think. To run her household well and smoothly without any of the conveniences that we now take for granted, she had to be sensible, efficient and hard-working, and usually she was all three. Nor was she always a housewife only. Then, as now, there were successful women writers, teachers, shopkeepers, and even reformers. There were women who earned their own livings and those of their families (2, 76), and others who followed their husbands through dangers and difficulties abroad. Brains, courage and initiative have never been the sole prerogative of the male sex in any age; and the names of many courageous and independent Victorian women—from novelists like Charlotte Brontë and George Eliot to reformers like Florence Nightingale and intrepid explorers like Mary Kingsley—immediately spring to mind. But the ordinary woman then had little encouragement to look outside her home, and as a rule she was quite content to remain there.

The comfortable security of mid-Victorian life was mirrored in the clothes that women wore(3, 7). They stood four-square in their billowing skirts and voluminous shawls, their feet encased in white stockings and thin slippers, or in short laced boots, and their serene faces framed in bonnets, or indoor caps of lace and ribbon. At the beginning of our period, crinolines (67, 127, 139, 140) were just coming into fashion. From about 1830 onwards, skirts had been growing steadily fuller; and by 1860 they had reached a truly enormous size. Many yards of material were needed for every dress; and, to support the weight, numerous starched petticoats were worn, with some-times a horsehair petticoat immediately beneath the skirt. Dressing in the morning must have been a lengthy business; for we are told that in 1856 a lady had daily to put on:

> long lace-trimmed drawers, an under petticoat three and a half yards wide, a petticoat wadded at the knees and stiffened in the upper part with whalebone, a white starched petticoat, with three stiffly starched flounces, a muslin petticoat, and finally the dress.[1]

[1] M. von Bohn, *Modes and Manners of the XIX Century.*

83 Bonnets and hats, 1848–96

The true crinoline, when it appeared about 1854, was a decided improvement on all this mass of underclothing. It was a sort of cage of steel and whalebone worn under the skirt, the weight of which it supported; and, awkward and cumbersome as it seems to us now, it was certainly better than the hot stuffy petticoats that had preceded it. It was not, however, always easy to manage. Even the smallest woman took up a great deal of room in a crinoline. Too rapid or hoydenish movements in such a wide skirt might easily mean upsetting some light piece of furniture, and sitting down carelessly sometimes made the skirt rise in an extremely awkward manner. The comic papers of the time were full of jokes about young women who were unable to get through narrow doorways or into carriages.

With these full-flounced skirts, tight-fitting bodices were worn, a short, tight jacket or a shawl, and a small bonnet or hat (83). The whole effect was rather like a full-blown rose held upside down. In the evening light, pale-coloured materials were often used; and some of the ball dresses of the time were charming. A young girl had to be plain indeed not to look attractive in a crinoline frock (67) of white or pink, fashioned in tarlatan, muslin, silk or lace, cut low at the neck and with short, puffed sleeves, the skirt flounced right up to the waist and trimmed with tiny wreaths of rosebuds or knots of ribbon. Her hair was worn in falling ringlets and sometimes crowned with a wreath of flowers; her stockings were of white or coloured silk; and her shoes were of soft kid, made without heels and secured by cross-bands over the foot. She carried a carved or inlaid fan, or a posy of flowers.

By day, heavier stuffs and cruder colours were general; and women showed a great fondness for tartans in rather violent shades. Until 1856 nearly all dyes were made from plants or mosses; but in that year a young man named W. H. Perkin made a remarkable discovery. He was only eighteen years old at the time, and was an assistant at the Royal College of Chemistry in London. One day, when he was experimenting with artificial quinine, he produced a dirty black powder that did not seem to be of any particular interest. He washed and liquefied it, however; and the totally unexpected result was a strong mauve dye.

This was the beginning of aniline dyes, produced from

84　Green cloth dress with green satin band, bow and sash, kilted cloth frills. Over-tunic and cuffs of green brocade. Green bonnet with white feather. 1878. *Le Journal des Modes.*

85　Cream voile dress with peacock-blue ribbons and lace at neck and sleeves. Straw hat with pink roses and peacock ribbons. 1884. *Myra's Journal.*

86　Walking dress of 1885. Jacket of brown corduroy velvet with painted mussel-shell buttons. Brown cloth dress. Bonnet of velvet, trimmed with lace and ostrich feathers.

mauve & blue

87　Blue dress with mauve bands, rosettes and zouave. White silk blouse and sleeves. Blue hat and mauve feather. 1893. *Le Journal des Modes.*

88　Purple cloth dress with black braid trimming, lace front and frill in sleeve. Shoe with patent toecap and white uppers. Black velvet hat with pink plume. White gloves. 1912. *Weldon's Ladies' Journal.*

84–8　Ladies' outdoor costume, 1878–1912

coal-tar, which we mentioned in Chapter V, where we wrote of William Morris. Perkin borrowed money from his father to set up a factory; and in a very short time the new purples became the rage. Gowns, gloves, hats, feathers, ribbons, all were purple; one writer in 1859 declared that "we shall soon have purple omnibuses and purple houses". Later experiments produced greens, blues, magentas and other shades; and the coal-tar industry was soon firmly established. At first the new shades were much harsher than those made from the old vegetable dyes; and, as a result, the fashionable Victorian lady went about in crude, staring colours that would now be considered in very bad taste.

Towards 1870 the long reign of the crinoline began to draw to its close. Women were tiring of their heavy flounced dresses, which made them all look alike and concealed a beautiful figure as completely as an ugly one. Skirts now became flat in front and bunched up behind(69). They were often double, the top part being looped up with large ribbon bows to show a lower skirt of contrasting colour. The width of the material was drawn round to the back and supported there by a small whalebone cage called a bustle. This was worn, like the crinoline, under the

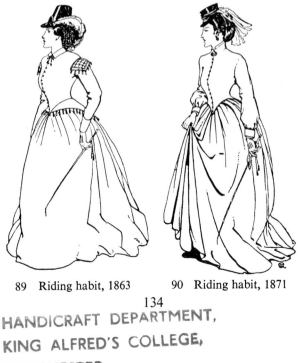

89 Riding habit, 1863   90 Riding habit, 1871

dress, and tied round the waist with tapes. The stuff flowed over it and downwards to the floor in a sort of cascade of drapery, which, for evening wear, usually ended in a beribboned and frilly train.

The bustle was really a modified form of crinoline, and the first step towards a simpler and more practical style of dress. About 1889 it disappeared, and thereafter skirts began to fit smoothly over the hips and to spread out into a bell-shape at the bottom. Waists were still narrow and bodices tight-fitting; but sleeves were beginning to expand. They gradually became bigger and bigger, until finally they swelled out into what was aptly nicknamed the "leg-of-mutton" style (7, 87). These sleeves were a very striking feature of fashionable dress in the nineties. Not only were they of enormous size; but frequently they were of different colour and even of different material from the rest of the garment. Women had ceased to look like inverted roses and now resembled two-handled vases in shape; but already their clothes were recognisably "modern", and were beginning to reflect the new ideas that were springing up all round.

The last quarter of the nineteenth century must have been a very stimulating period, especially for the young. Many important changes were on the way. New ideas of social reform, of manners, art and education were being eagerly discussed. For the first time in our history women were able to go to the Universities, like their brothers. It is true that, in those early years, only a very few girls actually went there, and most people still considered higher education unnecessary for their daughters; but a start had been made. It was no longer thought extraordinary or unsuitable for women to take an interest in outside affairs; and there was even some serious talk about women's suffrage.

In the world of sport and travel, too, horizons were broadening. Lawn tennis(91) was becoming very popular, and so was golf. In 1884 the safety-cycle appeared, which made it possible for women to bicycle—a sport they could not enjoy in the days of bone-shakers and penny-farthings. By 1896 the earliest motor-cars were to be seen on many roads—noisy and uncomfortable machines, much ridiculed by the horse-loving people of the time(116). All these developments encouraged people to move about and spend more time out of doors; and, like every change

91   Lawn tennis, 1883
By George Du Maurier

of any importance, they were mirrored in contemporary fashions.

The early woman motorist swathed her face and head in thick veils, covered her eyes with goggles, and wore a dust-cloak over her dress to protect it from the clouds of dust raised by the wheels. Needless to say, she was only a passenger: the woman driver was as yet unknown. As for the first female cyclists, they wore knickerbockers, with a mannish coat of the same material, and a small masculine-looking hat adorned with a little feather at one side. For summer days on the river or by the sea, high-necked, wide-sleeved blouses were worn, with small sailor hats of hard straw that were very like the "boaters" worn by men on the same outdoor occasions. The blouse, which for afternoon wear was fussy and frilly, was a development of the earlier garibaldi, a red shirt-like garment that had come into fashion when Garibaldi was fighting for Italian freedom, and which was an imitation, in finer material, of the coarse red shirts worn by his followers.

The knickerbockers favoured by early women cyclists were

136

not the earliest examples of these garments to be seen in Victorian England. In 1851 Mrs. Amelia Bloomer, an American, had caused much excitement by advocating what was then known as "rational dress". She contended, rightly enough, that the spreading skirts of the time were neither healthy nor economical, and that women ought therefore to abandon them and wear "pantalots", or long, full trousers tied at the ankles instead. Her followers were few in number; but they were extremely energetic and noisy. They held meetings in London and Dublin at which they appeared in the garments that were at once nicknamed "bloomers"; they preached their sartorial doctrine at every possible opportunity; and by way of making "rational dress" better known, they paraded the streets in twos, regardless of the hoots and jeers with which their appearance was greeted.

To the Victorians the idea of women in trousers was frankly shocking. Mrs. Bloomer was accused of trying to wreck home-life and of attempting to upset all the established customs of society. Abuse and ridicule were heaped upon the American and her disciples. Humorists made them the subject of countless cartoons; solemn articles filled with warnings and forebodings appeared in the newspapers; and coarse lampoons were sold by broadsheet vendors in the streets.

Public opinion, obviously, was not yet ready for "rational dress". But what really killed the new style, almost before it had begun to live, was not so much its alleged immodesty as its extreme ugliness. The sight of a woman in long bloomers below the waist and the ordinary jacket, bodice and hat of the period above it was enough to make anyone laugh, and to the Victorians the fashion seemed not only indecent but also highly ridiculous. The later cyclists' suits were a great improvement,

92 Yellow ninon tunic with ecru lace over yellow satin dress with small train and very narrow skirt. Mauve chiffon scarf and gold cord girdle. 1911. *Weldon's Ladies' Journal.*

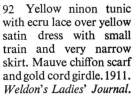

for coat, hat, and knickerbockers all matched, and so made a harmonious whole. But even they were short-lived; and it was to be many years before the idea of women in trousers or slacks became acceptable to the general public.

At the beginning of the twentieth century, clothes began to shrink in size. The bell-shaped skirt and the high-necked blouse remained in fashion until about 1908; and then the "hobble skirt" came in (88). This was an ankle-length garment so tight and narrow that it was almost impossible to hurry in it. A mincing gait was absolutely necessary; for, if the wearer attempted a longer stride, she either split her dress or was herself tripped up by it. As a slight relief, the skirt was sometimes slit a little way up one side to give greater ease in walking. Above these narrow, sheath-like dresses, were worn large flat hats with shallow brims, often heavily trimmed with flowers, feathers or ribbons.

It was the Great War of 1914 that swept away this inconvenient and top-heavy style, as it swept away so many better things. The last barriers that divided women from the outside world were then thrown down; and, instead of being encouraged to stay in the home, they were urged to come out and work. They were not "called-up" as they were in the second war; but volunteers streamed into the women's services, into munitions factories and offices, and on to the land. Even those who remained at home had far more work to do than before, for their maids left them to do war work, and the care of the house devolved upon them alone. They had no time for fine dressing; and all they wanted was something that would not hamper them in their labours and was quick and easy to slip on. So elaborate trimmings and fastenings disappeared for a time; hats grew smaller and dresses shorter; and, though smart and pretty clothes were still worn for formal occasions, the general styles were simple and workmanlike. Since those days we have seen many other changes in fashion, including the effects of another war and all the shortages that have followed it. But these cannot be discussed here; and we must wait to consider them until the history of our own lives, with all the striking changes that have occurred in them, comes to be written.

Chapter VIII

EDUCATION

THE Victorian child is popularly supposed to have led an extremely repressed and sober life, quite unlike that of children today. Most people, when they try to picture the nursery and schoolroom work of those days, think at once of numerous rules, prohibitions and punishments, of long, dull Sundays when no toys were allowed, and of stern parents who demanded absolute and unquestioning obedience to every command. In countless books about this period we are reminded that "Children should be seen and not heard", and "Spare the rod and spoil the child" were then favourite maxims; and we are sometimes given the impression that boys and girls went about more or less on tiptoe, hardly daring to play any noisy game, and certainly not daring to air their own views and wishes before mother or governess. In short, the general idea is that Victorian parents were mainly benevolent tyrants—kindly, of course, but far from sympathetic—and that children today are fortunate indeed not to have been born in those times.

In actual fact, much of this gloomy picture is exaggerated, and some of it is sheer nonsense. Victorian children were probably quite as happy and certainly as dearly loved as children in any other age. We can remember very clearly our own grandmother's tales of family life in the 'sixties, and how, as children, we listened with envy to her accounts of the freedom and comradeship enjoyed by a houseful of fifteen lively boys and girls. The family in question was a very ordinary one, neither rich nor distinguished; but its members had as good a time as anyone could desire. Most of their pleasures were home-made; but they were none the worse for that; and the accounts of picnics, explorations, parties and practical jokes, related by one who had taken part in them herself, presented a picture quite unlike that of the dull, almost grim homes in which some modern writers would like us to believe.

It is true that children in the mid-nineteenth century were more severely brought up than their present-day descendants.

139

Parents at that time took their responsibilities very seriously. A strong religious sense made them feel that every child was a sacred charge laid upon them by God, for whose spiritual and moral welfare they would one day be called upon to account. They believed it was their solemn duty to bring up each one first as a good Christian and then as a good citizen, and to this end everything in the family training was subordinated. Children were taught from a very early age that the most important things in life were duty and religion; and it was generally felt by all thoughtful people that to spoil a child unduly, or withhold punishment when it was needed, was not only weak-minded but definitely wrong.

In practice, this meant that instant obedience to every order, respectful manners and punctuality were expected as a matter of course from every member of the family. Argument and "answering back" were never permitted, and indeed they were seldom attempted, for parents then were regarded with a deep and genuine respect not untinged with fear. The father's word was law in nearly every family, and his authority was rarely disputed. As the breadwinner and legal head of the family, he was the pivot round which the whole house revolved. Next came the mother, and after her the governess or the nurse. Children came only fourth or fifth in the order of consideration, and they were certainly never encouraged to regard themselves as the centre of the household. The size of the average family alone would have made this quite impossible. Their parents were usually prepared to make the utmost sacrifices for their welfare if this was necessary. But, in theory at least, the children's wishes were only of secondary importance, and their opinions on any controversial domestic matter of no importance at all.

Early rising was an almost universal rule, with a correspondingly early bedtime at night. Many children were expected to practise on the piano for half an hour before breakfast, or to do their homework then; and, for this early-morning work, they often sat in unheated rooms even in winter. Good manners were considered especially important. Sons often addressed their father as "Sir". Little girls were trained to curtsey to visitors, and to stand with their hands folded when grown-up people spoke to them. Except during the children's hour before bedtime, when they could romp and chatter as much as they liked, children were not expected to speak in the presence of their parents until they were invited to do so. In practice, of course, they frequently talked a good deal, but one word from mother or father was enough to reduce even a lively chatterbox to cautious silence. Any lapse from decorum at table was immediately punished by a denial of pudding or, in more serious cases, by banishment to the nursery and a subsequent slapping.

Sunday was undoubtedly a very trying day for young people in the mid-Victorian period. This was not because it was universally regarded as a day of devotion and recollection, or because everyone went to church at least twice, in the morning and again in the evening. But unfortunately the day was made unnecessarily gloomy by an almost total prohibition of amusements, and even of the duller weekday occupations like sewing and mending. All shops and places of entertainment were, of course, closed, and no one travelled on Sundays except in cases of real necessity. It was usual for families to go for a walk together after morning service, and sometimes visitors were entertained to dinner or supper. This, however, was not very common, since it meant extra work for the servants, and it was the aim of every housewife to reduce the household tasks as far as possible on the day of rest. Week-end visits did not come into fashion until towards the end of the nineteenth century, when new ideas were stirring everywhere and the gloom of the Victorian Sabbath was beginning to lift a little.

Children went to the morning or evening service, and sometimes to both, and in some families they were sent to Sunday school as well in the afternoon. In the intervals they were expected to read religious books, and to repeat to their parents Collects previously learnt by heart or passages from the Bible and the Catechism. All toys and picture-books were locked away. Sometimes a Noah's Ark was allowed to the smaller children because it illustrated a Bible story, but dolls, hoops and painting-books had to wait until Monday. The older members of the family, too, were deprived of most normal occupations, for embroidery, games and music other than hymn-singing were all alike forbidden, and such worldly pleasures as cards or dancing were, of course, quite out of the question. Reading aloud from books of a devotional or improving character was a favourite Sunday diversion, and so was hymn-singing

141

round the piano. Apart from these, there was practically nothing to do.

Yet, despite all this, the average Victorian home was a pleasant and cheerful place to grow up in. If young people had to conform to more rules and conventions than are customary today, they were far from repressed, and decorum in the drawing-room was usually compensated by liveliness in the nursery. Life was made much easier by the fact that rents were low, and consequently it was possible to have a fair-sized house even with a comparatively low income. This meant that there was plenty of space to move about in, and rooms could be set apart for the children in which they could romp and play without annoying anybody.

In a large family there could be no lack of companionship, and numerous cousins, with whom visits were exchanged, added occasional variety. Each family tended to make a compact little world of its own, with its special private customs, jokes and games. Most of its amusements were home-made. At Christmas there might be a visit to the pantomime and a party or two(93), and in the summer there was a holiday by the seaside or a visit to an uncle's house in the country.

Good manners and the art of "give and take" were almost unconsciously learnt in a Victorian home. Awkward corners in the character were rubbed off in the rough and tumble of family life. Boys usually went to day- or boarding-schools as soon as they were old enough for serious lessons, or to some country rector who took a few pupils in his own home. School life was then considerably harder than it is today. Working hours were long and holidays short. The cane was often used, and there was a good deal of bullying in the more undisciplined schools. It was considered manly to be tough and hardy, and a delicate or nervous child must often have been very unhappy in his first term, before he had had time to accustom himself to the discomforts of his new surroundings.

The mid-Victorian period was a time of widespread educational reforms, most of which had been sorely needed. In the early nineteenth century some of the lesser boarding-schools were very rough-and-ready establishments, with insufficient and underpaid staffs. The ushers, or under-masters, were often incompetent, which is hardly surprising, since no capable man

93   A crowded, lively children's party, 1864
From "Bird's-eye Views of Modern Society", by Richard Doyle

would have accepted such poor pay as was then offered. The headmasters themselves were frequently more interested in making money from the catering charges than in the education of the children. The great public schools, of course, were better, for there was a long tradition of good teaching, and the boys who attended them were mainly from aristocratic families who paid high fees and expected the best in return. But even these schools had their barbaric side.

The grammar schools, too, had declined considerably since their foundation in Tudor or Stuart days; and most of the ancient Free Schools had sunk to a very low level. In one such school in Yorkshire the new rector found that the schoolmaster had been chosen, not for his qualifications as a teacher, but because he had failed as a farmer and must earn a living somehow. Those responsible for the appointment thought this a quite sufficient reason and were astonished at the rector's indignation; and probably there were many other schools up and down the country which were run on the same casual and peculiar lines.

But towards the middle of the century there was a general change of thought which resulted in widespread improvement. Old schools, both for day-boys and for boarders, were re-organised and brought up to date, and many new ones were founded. Much of this was due to the influence of that great man, Thomas Arnold, who became headmaster of Rugby in 1828. He was a man of deep religious feeling and eminent scholarship; and he dreamt of a school that should be the means of producing men of fine character and lively wits. He extended the rather narrow list of subjects that had previously been taught, and made the teaching interesting and alive, though he still gave the classics a more important place in the curriculum than modern languages, history or science. He established religion as a living force in the school, and trained the boys to work for the love of learning rather than from the dread of punishment. By the time he died, in 1842, Rugby had become one of the best schools in the country.

His example was widely followed thereafter by all the more progressive headmasters and school governors; and the result was a great increase in the popularity of boarding-schools. Other factors that contributed to this reformation were the spread of railways, which made travelling so much easier, and the general prosperity of the age, which enabled many more families to afford boarding fees for their sons. The existing schools were soon filled up, and there was a demand for new ones. It was at this period that many of the schools we know came into being, like Marlborough, which was started in 1843 for the sons of clergymen, and Wellington, founded ten years later for the children of Army officers.

A further important innovation was the rise and spread of preparatory schools, where boys were prepared for the big public schools. They are now so familiar a part of our educational pattern that it is sometimes difficult to remember that they scarcely existed before Victorian times. Quite small children used to be sent to public or private boarding-schools. Often they went at about eight or nine years old and remained there until they were old enough to leave school altogether. Sometimes they had two or three years at a small local school first; but usually they were thrown straight into the hurly-burly of public-school life without any more preparation than could be provided by a tutor or by their sisters' governess. Thomas Arnold was one of the first to recognise the disadvantages of this arrangement. He discouraged parents from sending boys to his own school until they were at least twelve years old, and it was he who encouraged the foundation in 1832 of Windlesham House, Brighton, the first English preparatory school run on more or less modern lines.

At the beginning of our period, girls were usually taught by governesses until they went to a finishing school; and many of them received their entire education at home. There were a few boarding-schools in existence that had not changed much since the start of the century; and of such establishments we read in Jane Austen's *Emma* and Thackeray's *Vanity Fair*. Finishing schools were chiefly concerned with accomplishments and deportment, and aimed at giving a final polish to young ladies before they took their place in the social world. Ordinary schools taught accomplishments also, and grounded their pupils in the simpler subjects without attempting to turn them into brilliant scholars. As yet only the most advanced thinkers dreamt of a university education for women.

Boys learnt Latin, Greek and higher mathematics; but ordinary people did not desire academic distinction for their girls. Indeed, too much learning was often regarded as a handicap to women, rather than an advantage. To be too clever was thought slightly unfeminine. Little girls acquired the rudiments of general knowledge from such text-books as *Magnall's Questions*, which dealt somewhat vaguely with anything from ancient history to the uses of whalebone, and from more valuable works that were read aloud to them while they sewed or netted purses. They learnt sufficient arithmetic to enable them to do their household accounts later on, but not, as a rule, algebra or geometry. It was considered essential that they should know how to sing, play and sketch a little, and for these subjects visiting masters were sometimes engaged if the governess was not capable of teaching them herself. They also learnt French and occasionally Italian, and a variety of handicrafts like tatting, netting, and woolwork. Above all, they were taught how to behave with decorum on every social occasion.

Games did not form part of feminine education, but dancing did, together with the art of curtseying gracefully in the long, full skirts of the period. Many children had to spend a certain time every day strapped to a backboard, so that they might grow up straight, or in walking about with a heavy book balanced on their heads, to acquire an easy carriage. Much attention was paid to plain sewing and embroidery. Children began at an early age to stitch laboriously on samplers(9) adorned with roses and pious mottoes. They learnt their letters and their needlework at the same time by embroidering the alphabet on long pieces of linen, and signing the work in cross-stitch with their names, ages and the date. "Honour thy Father and thy Mother that thy days may be long in the land" sewed little Mary Eltenton in 1849, when she was eight years old, and covered the rest of her sampler with well-shaped letters and numbers up to twelve. So many minute and even stitches must have taken a long time to do, and her eight-year-old fingers must have grown very weary before all was ended.

Yet, while countless little girls, with the complete approval of their parents, were being thus inadequately educated, far-reaching changes were taking place elsewhere. Great opportunities for women were already on the way; though it was not until some years later that the majority of daughters were allowed to profit by them. In Stuart times men and women had been equally well taught. Girls had learnt Latin, Greek and modern languages along with their brothers; the sons and daughters of the house shared the same tutor, and feminine education stopped short only at the gates of the University. In the eighteenth century a decline had set in. Now the pendulum was beginning to swing back.

The first difficulty that faced the reformers was to find a sufficient supply of competent teachers. Early Victorian governesses and schoolmistresses were rarely well paid; and often they had little real qualification for their task. A few were born teachers; but many undertook the work only because there was no other career open to them. Well-bred women did not earn their living unless they were forced to do so. Girls from poor families could go out as servants, shop-assistants or factory-hands; but the middle-class girl had to depend on teaching in private houses and schools, or on acting as companion to some elderly lady. Consequently, many daughters of impoverished houses became governesses regardless of whether or no they had the necessary gifts. It was not an easy life; but it was respectable and safe, and suitable posts were not too difficult to obtain.

Voluntary organisations like the National Society or the British and Foreign Schools Society had recognised the need for trained teachers quite early in the century, and had founded small colleges for both men and women students. But such teachers were mainly employed in the village schools maintained by these societies, and little was known about their colleges elsewhere. In 1848 a great step forward was taken by the foundation of Queen's College in London, and this was followed by the opening of Bedford College, also in London, in the following year. At the former were trained two very remarkable women who, in after years, were to be ardent educational reformers. They were Frances Mary Buss and Dorothea Beale, both of whom became headmistresses of schools quite unlike the usual academy for young ladies, and who believed that boys and girls were equally intelligent, and that the latter ought to have the same chances of development as their brothers.

Such ideas were not immediately acceptable in the first years of Queen Victoria's reign. Gradually, however, it dawned upon

147

94　Higher education for women, Girton College, Cambridge, 1877

all but the most old-fashioned parents that there was something to be said for these new notions. The advance began very slowly, but it was steady. In 1853 the Ladies' College at Cheltenham was founded, and five years later Miss Beale became its headmistress. This was the pioneer girls' boarding school of the new type, and by its success it exercised an enormous influence on the educational programmes of other schools.

In 1865 girls were permitted to sit for the Cambridge Local Examinations; in 1872 the Girls' Public Day School Trust was started, and its first schools opened in the following year. Little by little the old-fashioned seminary for young ladies gave place to schools with a wider curriculum and a healthier way of life, where games were played as a matter of course, and a variety of subjects were taught by highly trained teachers. By 1885 the modern type of girls' school was already on the way.

University education for women began in 1871, when Newnham College, Cambridge, was founded. Two years later Hitchin College was moved to Cambridge and restarted under the now familiar name of Girton (94); and in 1879 Lady Margaret Hall and Somerville were established at Oxford.

At first all these were very humble institutions, housed in private dwellings and having very few students. Women were not regarded as real members of the University, nor were they allowed to take degrees. They were there on sufferance only, and the utmost care had to be taken not to annoy or alarm the authorities. They were not allowed out alone in the town; when they went to lectures, they had to be chaperoned; and they scarcely ever spoke to a male undergraduate. But the mere fact that they were there at all showed how great an advance had been made since the early years of the nineteenth century. Then, one by one, the Universities granted membership and degrees to women. New colleges were built to house the increasing number of students, old restrictions were swept away, and finally complete equality was not only established but came, in time, to be taken entirely for granted.

While all these changes were taking place in the lives of well-to-do children, what was happening to the children of the poor? Here, too, the winds of reform were blowing strongly. During the first years of the nineteenth century, the poor child's lot was often very hard indeed, especially in the towns. Many were sent to work for long hours in mills and factories at a very early age (100). In mining districts they were employed to drag trucks of coal to the pit-mouth, or to sit all day in the dark, opening and shutting trapdoors for ventilation. In the country, boys began work as bird-scarers at seven or eight years old (95), and little girls helped their mothers to knit gloves, make

95 Boy bird-scarer, in a smock, with rattle, 1860
By John Leech

lace, or plait straw at home. They were more fortunate than the town child, for at least they were in decent surroundings and away from harsh and often brutal overseers. Conditions in Victorian factories were often very bad, even for adults; and for the very young they were terrible. For a child to work for ten hours or more in the noisy, damp, overheated atmosphere of a cotton mill, or in the darkness of a mine, was a dreadful thing, but it was then quite common, and few people thought it wrong or even undesirable.

We cannot altogether blame the parents; for many were then so poor that they could not afford to forgo the few pence the children could earn. Factory child-workers were paid about 4s. a week, or a little more. Country boys could earn from 1s. 6d. to 2s. 6d. a week, which, little though it now seems, was a considerable addition to the labourer's 7s. or 9s. wage. The temptation to add thus to the minute family income must have been strong; and it is enormously to the credit of the underpaid workers that they so often resisted it. Many made great efforts to send their children to the village school, thereby not only depriving themselves of extra money but sacrificing also a hard-earned penny or twopence a week in fees. There was far less excuse for the general public who, through lack of imagination and callousness, allowed thousands of children to toil like slaves.

Yet, if most people were indifferent, there were some who were not content to stand idly by. A succession of Factory Acts raised the age at which children could be employed and reduced their hours of work. Some of the worst abuses of the system were swept away by the Act of 1833, which not only forbade much that would seem horrible to us now but appointed inspectors to see that it did not occur. In the same year, Government grants were made to the two chief societies concerned with establishing schools for the poor. In 1842 little girls and women were forbidden to work in mines, and boys were not allowed down the pit until they were ten years old or more.

This was the beginning of better days for labourers' children; but much still remained to be done. Gradually the public conscience was stirred by the unremitting efforts of men like Lord Shaftesbury, Sir Robert Peel, and many others. "Deliver me these rickety, perishing souls of infants, and let your cotton trade take its chance," wrote Thomas Carlyle with bitter indignation in 1843. Thoughtful people understood that the health and happiness of children were of more value than any work they could do, and that their early years ought to be spent in schools, not in workshops. The battle raged for years; for it was not only the selfish and the careless who opposed the reforms. Some critics honestly believed it a natural thing for children to work for their keep as soon as they could, and that to forbid them to do so was an interference with the rights of parents. But these, happily, were on the losing side, and their numbers steadily waned as the years went by. The long fight was finally won in 1870, when the Government made education compulsory for all between the ages of five and fourteen.

Long before 1870, however, voluntary societies and single individuals had been striving to found and maintain schools for the poor, and to persuade parents to send their children there. Free Schools had existed for centuries in various parts of the country; and most villages had at least a dame-school in which labourers' children could learn reading, writing, and perhaps a little arithmetic. But as yet there was no uniformity of education, and little attempt was made to teach anything but the most elementary subjects. The old-established Free Schools had their own buildings; but the dame-schools were often housed in the front room of a cottage, a disused barn, or any other place that happened to be available. Teachers were hard to find; some were almost as ignorant as their pupils; and there was the further difficulty that attendance was not compulsory, which meant that children were often kept from school whenever the local farmers needed extra help in the fields.

It was the Churches, more than any other institutions, that set about remedying this state of affairs. Many parishes would have had no school at all had it not been for the generosity of the clergyman, who contributed largely to its upkeep and some-times supported it altogether. In some districts, landowners maintained schools at their own cost, or subscribed heavily towards them. Then, in 1811, the National Society was formed, and, three years later, the British and Foreign Schools Society.

In most of the pre-1870 schools, the parents paid a small fee of a penny or twopence a week; but in some very poor districts tuition was entirely free. The schools themselves varied considerably. Religion, reading, writing, arithmetic and needlework were the principal subjects taught in most; but some of the more ambitious masters went much further. At St. Mark's School, Lavenham, for instance, the Froebel System, which became so fashionable in the following century, was already in use as early as 1856. At Hitcham, in the same county, elementary science was taught by the rector, who was a professor of botany at Cambridge. He encouraged the children to take part in flower-shows, cricket matches, and other events hitherto unheard-of in connection with village schools. At Crosthwaite, Cumberland, dancing, singing, carpentry and gymnastics were encouraged; and here, too, there was a school garden, with beehives, and plants of all sorts. At St. George's, Bloomsbury, there was a boarding-school where seventy-five very poor children were housed; and at Ellesmere the vicar rented a house where fourteen boys lived and attended school every day.

Then there were the "half-time" schools for young men and boys who were already employed, and spent such free time as they had in learning. There were also industrial schools where particular trades or handicrafts were taught, such as carpentry, knitting or lace-making. And, in addition, there were, of course, Sunday schools, infant schools for the very young, and training colleges for teachers.

The Act of 1870 swept away the chief difficulty with which the voluntary societies and individuals had hitherto been faced, inasmuch as it obliged children to attend school regularly until they were fourteen years old, except in certain cases where particularly bright pupils were allowed to leave after they were eleven. Since that date, a variety of other Acts have widened the curriculum in primary schools, and provided more and more opportunities of higher, as well as elementary, education for all. Today every child, even the poorest, has the chance of going to secondary schools, and from thence to the University if he or she has the necessary aptitude. Much still remains to be done before England becomes a really well-educated nation. But, at least, the darkness of total ignorance has been dispelled; and it is mainly to the Victorians that we owe the solid foundations of our modern educational system.

Chapter IX

HEALTH

THE nineteenth century was a wonderful time for any doctor. Greater changes took place then, in medical science and practice, than during any previous period. Some of the age-old problems that had puzzled doctors for centuries were being solved at last, and others were being vigorously attacked by men who devoted their whole lives to study and experiment. On all sides, knowledge was advancing, and the basis of current medicine and surgery was being established.

One great change brought immediate relief from pain to thousands of patients who had to visit the dentist or face a surgical operation. Before the middle of the nineteenth century there were no anaesthetics of any kind, beyond a few inadequate drugs that dulled, but did not kill, the pain. When a man had a tooth out, he just had to grin and bear it; but when it came to major operations the patient needed rare courage; for there was no method of rendering him totally unconscious. He saw all the alarming preparations; he felt every movement of the knife. As a rule, he had to be tied down to the table to prevent him rolling about in his agony and making the surgeon's work impossible.

The first step towards an improvement had already been taken in the eighteenth century when laughing-gas, or nitrous oxide, was discovered, though hardly anyone realised its importance. This gas had the curious property of making those who inhaled it laugh immoderately and become extremely cheerful, excited and "outside themselves". Sir Humphry Davy(96), the inventor of the miner's safety lamp, was the first to notice that it also destroyed any feeling of pain. In 1824 Dr. Henry Hickman, of Ludlow in Shropshire, published the results of some experiments whereby he had succeeded in killing pain and producing unconsciousness for short periods. Nine years before, Michael Faraday had discovered that it was possible to produce the same effects with ether. But few people took these suggestions seriously; and, oddly enough, the earliest

96 Sir Humphry Davy
(1778–1829)
From a portrait after
Sir Thomas Lawrence

97 Michael Faraday
(1791–1876)
From an old photograph

use made of laughing-gas and ether was at parties, where people inhaled these drugs for the fun of the thing.

It was noticed, on one such occasion, that a man who had hurt himself apparently felt no pain when under laughing-gas. An American dentist named Horace Wells conceived the idea that this gas could be advantageous when extracting teeth. He experimented first upon himself; and, when he had had

98   The family doctor calls, 1861
By John Leech

a tooth drawn without feeling it, he delightedly declared that "a new era in tooth-pulling" had dawned. He was right; but, unluckily, he was not destined to convince the general public. At a demonstration held in 1844 he unfortunately used too little gas. The patient cried out in pain, and the spectators, not unnaturally, decided that the experiment had failed. Wells went on trying; but when a second demonstration failed he became discouraged and gave up dentistry.

His partner, William Morton, was made of sterner stuff; and, since laughing-gas seemed unreliable, he used ether successfully. Then he began experimenting on himself to see whether he could induce periods of unconsciousness long enough to permit of major operations. There was, of course, considerable danger, for, experimenting alone and unaided, he might easily have killed himself. But his reward came in 1846 when Dr. Warren of Massachusetts General Hospital performed the first big operation under ether. Two months later, an English surgeon, Robert Liston, operated on Frederick Churchill, a thirty-six-year-old butler, at University College Hospital, London, for a

155

thigh amputation, with Peter Squire as anaesthetist (99). Both these operations were completely successful. Churchill knew nothing about it from first to last, and when he came out of the anaesthetic he asked when the surgeons were going to begin. It is said that those who watched the proceedings felt the silence to be almost uncanny, so accustomed were they to the screams and groans of patients.

This, however, was only the beginning. There were still a great many difficulties to overcome. For one thing, ether as it was then, before it was refined and improved, was not an ideal drug. It was difficult to administer and its after-effects were bad. One old family doctor used to say a patient coming to after ether showed the effects of being blind drunk on bad whisky— very bad whisky. Many surgeons did not approve of it. It is possible that even after this encouraging start the science of anaesthetics might have waited for many years, had it not been for James Young Simpson (1811–70).

This great man was the Professor of Midwifery at Edinburgh. As a young man, he had studied medicine at that University, and had been severely tempted to take up some other profession, so great was the horror he felt at the agony of the patient at his first operation. Fortunately, he decided to go on with his studies, but to discover meanwhile some means of alleviating pain. He and two friends experimented constantly on themselves with all sorts of drugs. One day a chemist sent Simpson some chloroform, a drug discovered in 1831. The three men took it one evening. All were affected at once; but Simpson recovered first. He looked round the room and saw his colleagues lying unconscious under the table. Here, obviously, was something far better and stronger than anything tried before. In 1847 it was used with great success in a major operation on a Gaelic-speaking Highland boy, where Simpson administered the anaesthetic and Professor Miller removed part of the forearm bone (radius) for bone disease. From that time the science of anaesthetics became firmly established. The more old-fashioned surgeons were slow to use it; and Simpson had to overcome much opposition before his ideas were accepted at last.

Another wonder-working discovery concerned the use of antiseptics for surgical cleanliness. Today we take it for granted that every instrument is sterilised; every dressing, sponge and

156

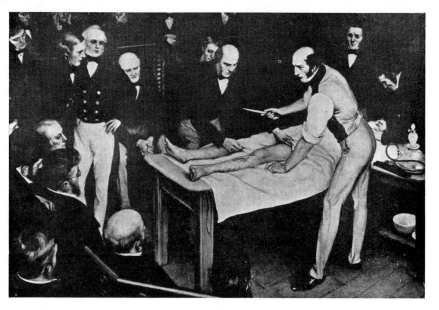

99 The first operation under an anaesthetic, by Robert Liston, in University College Hospital, London, December, 1846

100 Children working in a textile mill

bandage is kept free from the minutest particle of dirt or infective matter. Surgeons and nurses are dressed in spotless clothes, and even wear masks during operations. And the same scrupulous cleanliness is enforced while the wound is being dressed and tended during its slow healing.

A little more than a hundred years ago, such precautions were unknown. Surgeons usually wore some old, spotted, blood-stained coat that could not be spoilt; some made no further preparation than a perfunctory washing of their hands; and a few did not trouble to do that. In the hospital wards, too, the standard of cleanliness was low. The rooms were swept and scrubbed, of course; but no real attempt was made to keep everything pure and spotless. As a result, many patients died of gangrene; and hundreds of lives were lost even after successful operations.

This state of affairs existed because no one then knew why wounds turn septic. The minute organisms that produce infection had not yet been discovered; and the terrible waste of life due to what was then known as "hospitalism" was the despair of every doctor. It was left to a great Frenchman, Louis Pasteur, to lead the way in a hitherto-unknown science called bacteriology, and by his discoveries and experiments lead to the modern antiseptic system.

Pasteur was a tanner's son from the Jura who, in 1854, became Professor of Chemistry at Lille. He was an exceedingly brilliant man, who had already made his name by discovering the crystal formation of tartaric acid; and, while at Lille, he tackled the problem of why wine and milk turn sour. He found that it was due to the action of micro-organisms, and that this could be prevented by what we now call "pasteurisation", or the application of heat. But this solution did not satisfy his ardent curiosity; and he set out to discover whence these organisms came. Eventually, he found that they existed in the air, and that, by settling in wine or milk, they produced chemical changes that resulted in fermentation.

This discovery was of enormous value to wine-makers and dairy farmers; but the story did not end there. The great English surgeon, Joseph Lister, had been studying the problem of wound infection for years, and had already begun to suspect that this was caused by something in the air, when his attention was

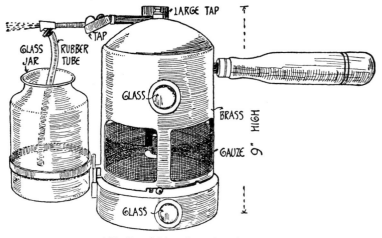

101 Lord Lister's antiseptic spray
Royal College of Surgeons Museum, London

drawn to Pasteur's work. This gave him the lead he wanted. He saw that if minute airborne organisms could cause fermentation in liquids they might also cause infection in wounds, and the first thing necessary, therefore, was to exclude them from the patient's body.

For this purpose he started, in 1865, to use carbolic acid in dressings; and he also insisted that instruments, and the surgeons' fingers, should first be treated with the same disinfectant. He invented a lamp that sprayed carbolic all over surgeons, nurses and patient during operations (101, 102). In a long operation, those present were often wet through before it ended; but an antiseptic atmosphere was thus created.

In the wards, too, he insisted upon meticulous cleanliness. Two of his favourite sayings were: "Success depends upon attention to detail," and "There is only one rule of practice: put yourself in the patient's place!" All this, of course, was something quite new in hospital methods; and it was a long time before his ideas were generally accepted. Old-fashioned surgeons were inclined to laugh at Lister's theories, and regard them as so many newfangled fads. But it was noticed that his patients recovered, whereas those of other surgeons died. Little by little, the use of antiseptics spread, better and stronger

102   Operation of 1880 with Lister spray in use
From "Antiseptic Surgery", by W. Watson Cheyne

materials were employed, and the rules governing their use in hospitals became more strict, until to-day the standard is far higher than anything of which Lister ever dreamt. Thousands of lives were saved thereby; and, when Lister died in 1912, the Royal College of Surgeons' Report contained the following tribute: "His work will last for all time; humanity will bless him evermore and his fame will be immortal." And the same can truly be said of Louis Pasteur.

Pasteur's services to the human race, however, did not end with his work on micro-organisms. Besides conquering various animal plagues and discovering a remedy for hydrophobia, that terrible and hitherto incurable disease caused by the bite of a mad dog, he made another great contribution to health by devising a method of purifying sewage. He found that harmful waste materials could be cleaned by anaerobic organisms, which only work in the absence of oxygen, and by other aerobic organisms that work in the open air. Both were necessary for complete purification. Pasteur therefore invented a process whereby sewage was first broken up in a closed tank and then passed through trickling filters (104). In this way it could be discharged with safety into rivers, estuaries, and the sea.

Before the nineteenth century and, indeed, for many years afterwards, sanitary arrangements in England, as in other countries, were extremely primitive. Sewers existed in most towns; but there was no main drainage system. Many houses were still without water-closets, though these were introduced in the late eighteenth century and were slowly becoming popular. Where they did not exist, an earth-closet in the garden was used, with a cesspool below which was cleaned out from time to time. The sewage filtered away into the ground and was

160

purified as it went by the earth. There was a danger that surface water might get in and, percolating through the soil, affect the water supply; but, on the whole, the system worked comparatively well except where too many houses crowded together.

Later on, however, when the towns began to spread rapidly, the old cesspools no longer sufficed, and it became necessary to connect them with the town sewers. These discharged into small streams, many of which were bricked over to act as drains, and so, *via* these streams, into the main river or the sea. The result was that rivers became polluted. In Elizabethan and Stuart times, the Thames had been London's main highway, along which men travelled constantly for business or for pleasure, and in which people fished and bathed in safety. During Queen Victoria's reign, that was no longer possible. At low tide the river stank. The salmon that had once been caught in it had long since disappeared and anyone bold enough to bathe in it ran the risk of being poisoned. Great stretches of foul-smelling mud lay along the banks; and, in the House of Commons, Members complained that they could not use the rooms overlooking the water because of the appalling stench.

Nor was this the worst. The untreated sewage that flowed into

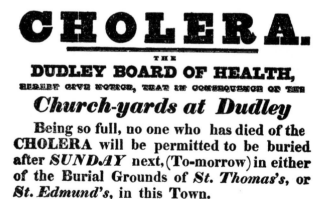

CHOLERA.

THE
DUDLEY BOARD OF HEALTH,
HEREBY GIVE NOTICE, THAT IN CONSEQUENCE OF THE
Church-yards at Dudley
Being so full, no one who has died of the CHOLERA will be permitted to be buried after *SUNDAY* next, (To-morrow) in either of the Burial Grounds of *St. Thomas's,* or *St. Edmund's,* in this Town.

All Persons who die from CHOLERA, must for the future be buried in the Church-yard at Netherton.

BOARD of HEALTH, DUDLEY.
September 1st, 1832.

W. MAURICE. PRINTER. HIGH STREET. DUDLEY.

103 Handbill on the burial of cholera victims,
Dudley, Worcestershire
From "Dudley", by Chandler and Hannah

161

the river was responsible for horrible outbreaks of disease. In 1848, and again in 1853, cholera swept over London like the Plague of earlier times, coming up the river and killing thousands of men, women and children. The germ of cholera was not discovered until 1884, when Robert Koch, a German doctor, who also discovered the bacillus of anthrax and the tubercle bacillus and greatly advanced the treatment of tuberculosis, succeeded in identifying it. But already scientists had learned that cholera was waterborne, a fact established by John Snow, whom we have met as a pioneer in anaesthetics; and in 1855 Sir John Simon set himself to overcome the perils that came from London's contaminated river.

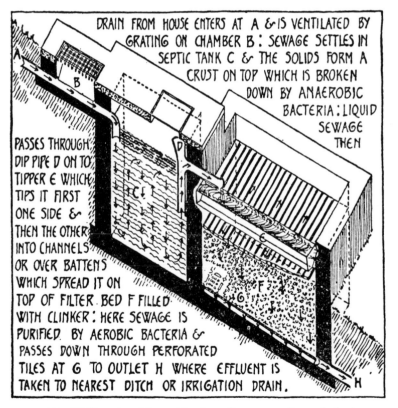

104   Half-sectional isometric view of a sewage disposal plant
for a small house

Simon was the first Medical Officer of Health for the City of London. Appointed in 1848, he began at once to cope with the twin problems of water supply and sewage disposal. His reports to the City Council were full of scathing comments upon the dreadful conditions that prevailed. Until he retired in 1876, he said what he thought quite fearlessly. He appointed sanitary inspectors, then known as Inspectors of Nuisances. He was perpetually preaching the need for cleanliness, and did everything possible to convince the general public that insanitary ways were not only unpleasant but dangerous. And he demonstrated that pure water was of primary importance by showing that, where water was taken from an unpolluted part of the river, the deaths from cholera were only 37 in every thousand, while in contaminated areas they were as high as 130 a thousand.

His vigorous criticisms eventually roused the Government. By 1865 a complete main drainage system had been built in London, and similar enterprises were begun in other towns. The actual engineering work was carried out by Sir Joseph Bazalgette; and the great part he played is sketched in Vol. III. Pasteur's purifying methods were generally adopted. In 1876 the Rivers Pollution Prevention Act forbade the discharge of untreated sewage into any stream.

Great changes were also taking place in the nursing profession. Nurses did not formerly receive the long and careful training that they get today; they were often rough and ignorant women, poorly paid and usually overworked. Little more was required of them than that they should be strong, willing, of good character, and able to carry out simple instructions. Some of the women were incompetent and idle, and a few disreputable; and nursing was not considered a suitable career for educated girls.

Simple ailments were usually treated at home, and most housewives had some acquaintance with nursing and first-aid. Nursing homes did not exist; and no one went to hospital if he or she could be looked after elsewhere. This is scarcely surprising when we remember what the hospitals were like. In workhouse infirmaries, even the rough-and-ready services of half-trained nurses were lacking. The poor were looked after by old and incompetent inmates of the institution. The Army itself had no organised Medical Corps, but depended upon doctors attached to different regiments, upon "Apothecaries to the Forces", who

163

were chemists in charge of stores and equipment, and upon nursing orderlies, who were pensioners, or soldiers not strong enough to fight.

It is to a woman that we owe the enormous changes in the nursing service. Florence Nightingale was born in 1820, the daughter of a Derbyshire landowner. From her early youth, she was passionately interested in medical matters. She greatly desired to be a nurse, but her parents were strongly opposed to the idea. Well-to-do girls did not normally enter professions. Moreover, there was no place in England where she could be trained. She was thirty years of age before she finally won permission to go to Kaiserswerth, in Germany, for training. During the next ten years she became not only a fully qualified nurse but a competent hospital manager.

When the Crimean War broke out in 1854, women were not employed in military hospitals. At Scutari, the main hospital, into which poured an enormous number of wounded, conditions were appalling. There were not enough orderlies, the equipment was bad and insufficient. The wards were horribly overcrowded; there was a lack of proper dressings and instruments; and food was often short. Faced by this problem, Sidney Herbert, the Secretary at War, took the then revolutionary step of asking Florence Nightingale to go out with 150 women nurses and endeavour to bring some order out of confusion. Accordingly she left England with a mixed party of nuns and secular nurses, and duly arrived at Scutari after a storm-tossed voyage.

On landing, she found that she was far from welcome. The more old-fashioned doctors resented women nurses, and were eager to pounce upon and make the most of any mistake. It needed the utmost tact to overcome their opposition. Gradually, however, the valuable work they did recommended them to even the most hidebound doctors; while their presence in the wards saved the lives of hundreds of wounded men. Order and good organisation took the place of muddle and carelessness; and, in a few months, the overcrowded hospital became a real place of healing instead of an ante-room to the morgue. The war lasted only three years, but this was long enough to convince the public that never again must soldiers be without proper medical organisation. In 1857 the first Army Hospital Corps was formed, and in 1898 the Royal Army Medical Corps came into being.

FLORENCE NIGHTINGALE

When Florence Nightingale returned to England, she found herself a national heroine. She devoted the rest of her long life to ensuring that there would always be a contingent of skilled nurses available. A large fund was raised for her in token of the nation's gratitude, and this she used to endow a school for nurses at St. Thomas's Hospital. Other training schools were established, so that English women who wished to take up nursing were no longer obliged to study abroad.

Florence Nightingale lived over fifty years after her return from the Crimea, till she died in 1910 at the age of ninety. She had not only established the status of the nurse; it is probably largely due to her influence that the English soldier came to be regarded as an excellent fellow and fine fighter rather than a drunken lout. Other women were inspired by her example. One, known and loved throughout Liverpool as Sister Agnes, became head of the Training School for Nurses of the Poor there. She it was who first persuaded the Poor Law Authorities that it was only right to have properly trained workers to look after workhouse inmates. When she first began her campaign in Liverpool Workhouse, that dismal institution was full to overcrowding, owing to the American Civil War and the consequent cotton famine. The lack of raw cotton from America threw thousands out of work, and, without unemployment insurance, they were driven to the workhouse. For many the sad move to the infirmary was their last move on earth.

In 1849, an even stranger portent appeared on the medical horizon—that hitherto unheard-of creature, a woman doctor. In the past, country-wise women had often been consulted for minor ills; and, though many of their remedies were mere superstitious mumbo-jumbo, they were not without much useful knowledge. But that a woman should spend years in training, and mix with rough medical students, was a development that at first appeared exceedingly distasteful. Nevertheless, in 1849, Elizabeth Blackwell, a native of Bristol, received her medical degree in New York; and, during the following year, a women's medical college was founded in Pennsylvania, the first school of medicine entirely for women.

No doubt many old-fashioned English people felt that such a thing could happen in America, but never in England. Once again, critics were proved wrong. Dr. Blackwell returned to

England and practised there. She also gave lectures in London; and, at one of these, a young girl, afterwards famous as Elizabeth Garrett-Anderson, was a member of the audience. She made up her mind that she, too, would be a doctor. Enormous difficulties had to be overcome, including the disapproval of her friends, and the fact that women were debarred from all recognised medical schools. But the Society of Apothecaries could not, by their Charter, prevent her from taking their examination; and this she did in 1865, passing with credit and obtaining the diploma that permitted her to practise.

Immediately the Society altered its regulations, so that no more women could be admitted; but this was shutting the stable door after the horse had been stolen. There were now two women doctors practising, and others were soon to follow. In 1869, Sophia Jex-Blake and six other women applied to the University of Edinburgh for medical training and were admitted. Yet the opposition to women doctors was still very strong. The male students hated and resented them. At Edinburgh, the female students were separately taught and were not allowed the same status; and on one occasion there was an ugly riot, when mud and filth were thrown at the unfortunate women.

But, very slowly, the position improved. Elizabeth Garrett-Anderson founded St. Mary's Hospital for Women (now called, after her, the Elizabeth Garrett-Anderson Hospital). In 1874, the London School of Medicine for Women was opened; and finally, in 1892, the British Medical Association admitted women as members.

As the nineteenth century wore on, more and more efforts were made to prevent disease, rather than deal with it once it had broken out. The Government recognised that the health of the nation was one of its most important concerns; and numerous Acts of Parliament were passed to enforce better conditions of housing, sanitation, water supply and ventilation. In 1875, the Public Health Act made it compulsory for every rural or urban area to have its Medical Officer of Health. Later Acts provided for the inspection of food supplies and the isolation of infectious cases, for the regular medical inspection of school-children, and for the better control of consumption and other diseases.

With the discovery by Wilhelm Conrad Rœntgen of X-rays in

1895, the work of healing bone fractures was greatly advanced. Many a patient who might in earlier years have been a cripple for life was saved from such a fate because for the first time the surgeon could actually see through the flesh and muscle to the broken bone beneath. Later, X-rays were used to diagnose lung and brain lesions, and also internal diseases of various sorts. X-rays were then employed in attacking skin diseases. It was found, if used without proper precautions, they may cause skin cancer in the operator; but deep X-ray application is often effective in the treatment of malignant growths.

Often a cause of serious trouble was the patient's unwillingness to go to the doctor in time; and the first step towards solving this problem was taken in 1911, when the National Insurance Act was passed, which made it compulsory for every employed person to contribute a few pence as an insurance from his weekly wages. The employer also paid a contribution, and the balance was supplied by the Government. The insured patient had no doctor's bill to meet, and sickness benefit was paid during absence from work.

At the time, this seemed a revolutionary idea; but, in fact, it was not so novel as many people supposed. As long ago as 1785, the Reverend John Acland, Rector of Broadclyst, Devon, had drawn up a scheme on much the same lines. This was embodied in a Bill introduced in Parliament in 1787; but, unfortunately, nothing came of it. The 1911 Act was only a beginning. It did not include dental services, or certain other forms of treatment. Today we have a free medical service that covers every form of doctoring and dentistry. We have also an active Ministry of Health, set up in 1919, which administers the funds derived from taxation for health purposes, and is responsible for the health and well-being of the entire nation.

Chapter X

TRANSPORT: ROADS AND RAILWAYS

THE first fifty years of Queen Victoria's reign might well be called the Age of Railways; for it was during that period that this comparatively new method of transport really came into its own. Railroads themselves—that is to say, tracks with wooden or iron rails laid upon them—were, of course, not new. They had been known at least as early as the sixteenth century and were frequently found in coal-mining districts, where loads of coal were drawn along them from the pithead to some convenient river or seaport. There were, naturally, no locomotives on these early tracks; the wagons were horse-drawn, and the sole reason for rails was to lighten the strain on the horses; and to enable them to move larger consignments in a single journey.

There is a brief account of the beginnings of railways in Vol. III of *Everyday Things*; and more recently the story of our railways has been told in greater detail by Mr. O. S. Nock in his fascinating book *The Railways of Britain*. This tells a story of struggle and achievement that everyone should read; for England was the great pioneer in railway construction and running. All we can do in a backward glance is to refer to the pioneer work on engines of Richard Trevithick, and the great formative achievements of George Stephenson, who was concerned with the famous Stockton and Darlington line, the first public steam railway in the world, opened in 1825. Stephenson's *Rocket* won the £500 prize at the Rainhill trials in 1829; and in 1830 the Liverpool and Manchester railway was opened, after extraordinary difficulties had been overcome in carrying the line over five and a half miles of the quaking bog called Chat Moss.

New lines sprang up all over the country; and by 1845 a positive "railway fever" had gripped the realm. Scores of short tracks were built, each with its separate company, and with varying gauges that in many cases made it impossible to use the rolling-stock of one on the lines of another. The broad gauge of 7 feet was favoured by the great engineer Brunel (105), adopted

168

105 Isambard Kingdom Brunel, standing in front of the anchor chain of the
Great Eastern
From a photograph taken in the 'fifties

by the Great Western Railway, and not entirely discarded until 1892. Stephenson preferred the narrow gauge of 4 feet 8½ inches; and, eventually, this became the standard for the whole kingdom. The majority of the early lines were intended only to connect two different towns, like the Liverpool and Manchester Railway, the Leicester and Swannington, and many others. But, in 1837, the first long-distance route came into being, when the newly opened London and Birmingham Railway linked up with the Liverpool and Birmingham, and thus made it possible to travel directly from London to Lancashire. By the start of our period, the railway systems of England were beginning to bear a recognisable resemblance to the systems that we know today; but many years passed before the little local lines had all been absorbed into six or seven great cross-country organisations.

Old gentlemen might deplore the noise and dirt of railways and tremble at their excessive speed; but for the young, the busy and the adventurous, it was both thrilling and convenient to whirl along at twenty miles an hour, and see the countryside from a totally new and unaccustomed angle. They travelled in what we should now consider very uncomfortable conditions. The carriages were unheated and badly lit; and only first-class passengers could depend on being completely sheltered from wind and rain. Some second-class compartments had walls only up to the waist, while the third-class were open to the sky and had hard wooden benches for seating. On the Greenwich line, third-class passengers in 1839 had to stand all the way from London Bridge, and were charged 6d. each for the privilege of doing so. Even twenty miles an hour might well seem an excessive speed in these conditions, with the wind whistling in one's face and rain or snow beating upon unprotected heads, not to mention the constant shower of smuts and sparks from the engine. But gradually conditions improved. The open or half-walled carriages disappeared; and by 1868 we find padded seats, painted woodwork and gas lamps well established.

All this was not achieved without violent opposition from landowners, farmers and sportsmen. Landowners charged very high prices to the hated companies, and hedged each sale of land with every restriction that they could devise. The London, Chatham and Dover Railway, in 1863, was obliged to build a long viaduct near Herne Hill because the Governor of Dulwich

College said that an embankment would spoil the village. Important towns refused to have the railway at any price, which explains why some quite large towns are not on the main line today, but connected with it by a branch line. Northampton was one of these; Windsor was another. The authorities of Eton College were able to secure a clause forbidding the Great Western Railway to build a station at Slough; but there the Company were too clever for them. They did not construct a station; but the trains stopped at Slough nevertheless, and the sale of tickets and other business was carried on at a nearby public house.

In the sixty-three years we cover, there were great changes in the design and development of railway engines. For a decade or so after 1851, we find antique-looking locomotives, such as the two-coupled "Copper Nob" type on the Furness Railway, little different from the Liverpool and Manchester "Lion" of 1838. These engines had inside cylinders; but there were a number of outside cylinder designs with single front wheel and coupled driving-wheels such as Beatty's *Herod* of the South-Western Railway in 1865 (106). There were also many single-wheeler engines—Beatty's *Eugenie* of the same line in 1857. Gradually, during the 'seventies, the boiler became larger and higher, the long funnel was shortened; and by 1880 we notice mixed traffic engines with coupled driving-wheels and outside frame, the charming single-wheels of the Brighton and South Coast Railway ("Gladstone" type 2-2-2, 1880), earlier the Great Western Railway broad gauge 4-2-2, non-bogie, and, most graceful of all, Stirling's Great Northern 8-foot single-wheelers (4-2-2), remarkable for their high speed.

So progress continued, with larger designs and higher boilers, with leading bogie and large coupled driving-wheels, later lengthened by a trailing-wheel (the so-called "Atlantic" type), till the introduction of the "Pacific" type with triple-coupled driving wheels, both with outside cylinders and both dated about 1900. The Walschaert valve gear was introduced about 1911 and was standard on several English railways, though not all. The Great Northern even added a trailing-wheel to some of their "Pacific" types (4-6-2) to make the largest standard engines on English railways. In addition, there were four-coupled goods engines (2-8-0), with large tank engines (e.g. 4-4-2, 2-6-2 and 2-6-4) for suburban and branch lines.

106 Joseph Beattie's *Herod*, 2-4-0; it ran on the London and South Western Railway from 1865 to 1890

107 The first English dining-car, on the Great Northern Railway, 1879

With goods trains, the wagon shows very little change throughout our period; but the Victorian age witnessed the introduction of special vans for fruit, meat and fish, some of a refrigerating type. Passenger rolling-stock gained enormously in spaciousness and comfort, principally towards the end of the century. We have noted that seats came to be padded and cushioned; but England was slower in adopting corridor trains. A complete set of corridor coaches started in 1892 from London to Glasgow; but the first restaurant car preceded the corridor, and was introduced in 1879, on a very ornate American model (107). For many years oil-lamps lighted the carriages, until at length gas-light took their place; and only within the memory of middle-aged people were trains equipped with electric bulbs; while metal foot-warmers, distributed by porters at the terminus, were replaced by modern steam-heating.

The most serious opposition was from the coach-owners, who rightly foresaw financial ruin. But nothing could hold the railways back; and the bustling, picturesque life of the roads came

108 A hansom cab, 1867
By John Leech

173

to an abrupt conclusion. Where a dozen or more coaches had clattered every day into a single town; where scores of ostlers and serving-maids, cooks and scullions had worked hard and fast to feed hungry passengers and horses during their brief halt; where countryfolk had waited impatiently for the goods, letters and news brought by the coach, and children had turned out to wave to it as it rumbled through little villages with jingling harness and sounding horn—all now was silence and desolation. The inns that had once been England's pride sank into mere local meeting-places; the coachmen and guards drifted away to less congenial employment, and many of the coach-owners found that they were faced with bankruptcy. Almost every great advance brings with it hardships; but few developments have brought such changes into so many lives as did the advent of the railways.

Temporarily, except for local traffic, the roads that threaded the country were almost deserted. Farmers' carts and carriers' wagons still used them, of course; and so did horsemen riding on business or pleasure, and the carriages of the gentry. But these made only comparatively short journeys from one country house to another, to the market town for shopping, or from the

109   Paying Calls in a brougham, 1869
By John Leech

farm to the village and the nearest station. For long distances travellers now used the railway; and it seemed obvious, at that time, that the highly organised road transport industry, which for two centuries had provided employment for so large a number of the population, had finally passed away, never to return.

In towns, naturally, there was as much traffic as ever (5, 113). The streets were filled with cabs, omnibuses and horse-drawn trams, as well as with private carriages (109), tradesmen's vans, and butchers' errand-boys dashing about on horseback with their laden baskets. Victorian cabs were of two kinds—the four-wheeler or "growler", which carried four passengers, and the hansom cab, which carried two (108). The latter was named after a cab invented by Joseph Hansom in 1834; but it differed considerably from the original design. The driver sat high up at the back of the vehicle, with the reins passing through a support on the front of the roof. He communicated with his passengers through a small trap in the top of the cab. The front of the hansom was open, except for two folding doors which came about half-way up and protected the travellers' feet and legs against the weather. To ride in a well-kept cab of this type, with its brightly polished lamps and brass work, its jingling harness and smartly trotting horse, was a very pleasant experience. The hansom cab was very popular in its own day, especially with young people; and there were many who deeply regretted its disappearance when it was finally driven off the streets by the modern taxicab.

Tramways were introduced into this country by an American named G. F. Train. The first public tramline in Europe was opened in Birkenhead in 1858; and from that Cheshire port they spread, slowly and after many setbacks, to most of the chief English cities. Unlike the buses of the time, the early tramcars had no upper decks. They ran along the raised outer edges of iron plates laid level with the road surface; and it was the consequent rigidity of their course that provided the strongest argument against them. Being unable to swerve like other vehicles, they often caused traffic blocks in busy streets; and, even in the heyday of the electric tram, this remained a serious drawback. Towards the end of the century, continuously running cables, worked by steam, were sometimes used instead

175

110 A "penny-farthing"; front wheel
58 in. diameter, 1884
Science Museum, London

of horses, especially in hilly districts; and experiments were also made with steam and with compressed-air power. But it was not until wholesale electrification became possible that tramways really became popular; and then, for a time at least, they were to be found in almost every town of any size.

Omnibuses first appeared in London in 1829; and by the beginning of our period they were already well established both there and in most provincial centres. The mid-Victorian bus carried twelve passengers inside and ten out; the upper deck was reached by narrow iron steps with handrails, and was provided with a kind of double bench, known as the "knifeboard", on which passengers sat back to back, facing the pavement on either side (113). There were also two seats next to the driver, which were much prized by young men. A handrail ran around for safety; but at first this had no boards beneath it, so that the passengers' legs and feet were visible from the street below. Because of this, and also because of the extreme difficulty of negotiating the ladder with decency in a wide skirt, it was not considered suitable for women to ride on the top of an omnibus until about 1883, when the "knifeboards" were abolished in favour of forward-facing garden-seats, "decency boards" were built along the sides, and a staircase was substituted for the awkward iron ladder.

We can see a typical inside in Egley's masterly painting (112), which shows, incidentally, that the vehicle was used by all classes. The floor was covered with straw, which kept the feet warm in winter but was decidedly awkward if one dropped a coin or some other small and easily lost object. The only light was a dim oil

176

111 A traction engine in a country lane, 1884

112 Inside a bus, dated 1859
From the painting by W. Maw Egley, on loan at the Tate Gallery

lamp near the entrance, by which the conductor did his accounts at night. Neither he nor the driver had any shelter against the weather. The driver had a slanting, unroofed seat on the box, into which he was strapped by a belt hooked over a post behind him. The conductor stood on a small platform, also unroofed, which jutted out from the rear of the bus, near which was an iron handle or a strap that helped him to steady himself when the bus was moving.

Apart from public transport, the most usual method of covering short distances was in a private carriage (5, 109), or on horseback. The most popular carriages were the victoria (5), named after the Queen; the brougham (109), named after Lord Chancellor Brougham, who is said to have invented it; the single landau, the phaeton, and the dogcart. About 1868 a new and very peculiar machine appeared on the roads (115). This was the "boneshaker", the forerunner of the modern bicycle. It was

113   Omnibuses of "knifeboard" type, at 9 a.m. at
the Bank of England, 1862
By W. McConnel

178

114 The "Coventry" tricycle for sedate riders, 1876

Science Museum, London

followed by a truly perilous contraption with a small wheel at the back and a very large one in front(110), known as the "penny-farthing", and later on as the "ordinary" bicycle, to distinguish it from the then newly invented safety machine.

It was not the first bicycle to be seen on our roads. A wooden machine had been known as early as 1839; and something rather like an elaborate hobby-horse had been used still earlier. But the mid-Victorian "boneshaker" was made of iron and steel and had solid or cushion rubber tyres(115). Mounting the "ordinary" or "penny-farthing" was not at all an easy business. The rider had to rest one foot on the step and hop along the ground till the bicycle had gained sufficient speed; then he sprang lightly—and not always successfully—into the high saddle. Obviously, such a machine was impossible for women in long skirts and crinolines, and cycling consequently was a purely masculine pastime for many years.

It was the invention of the safety bicycle, with a comparatively low seat and equal wheels, that gave women and elderly people the freedom of the roads. A lady's bicycle was

115 Coasting downhill on a "boneshaker", 1869; front wheel 36 in. diameter

Science Museum, London

179

produced without the horizontal bar; and on this women bowled along country roads with their brothers, or circled round and round the London parks. Towards the end of the nineteenth century, cycling became intensely popular with every sort of person. There were schools that taught the art, like the Royal Cycle Riding School in Euston Road, London. Young men and maidens formed touring parties and organised picnics at weekends and holidays; and before long bicycles began to be used for business as well as pleasure, by labouring men going to their work, by messengers and errand-boys, and by carriers of light goods.

An invention far more important in the history of road transport also came into prominence about this time. In 1885 Benz constructed his first motor-car; and during the same year Daimler produced a motor-cycle driven by petroleum vapour. Two years later the first petrol-driven car was built, again by Daimler.

Even before this, the "horseless carriage" was by no means a new or unheard-of notion. In 1800 an inventor named Medhurst had patented an engine worked by gunpowder that was designed to move carriages. In 1803 a steam omnibus, with a maximum speed of ten miles an hour, was actually seen in the streets of London, though it disappeared very quickly because the authorities refused to license so alarming a vehicle. But it was the internal combustion engine that launched the motor industry as we know it today; and, with its appearance, a new chapter began in the long history of road travel.

France was the pioneer country where this new invention was concerned. By 1891 cars were already running on her roads, erratically, no doubt, and with speeds hardly more than those of smartly trotting horses, but nevertheless as an accepted part of the ordinary traffic. In England, progress was greatly hampered by an antiquated law that forbade any mechanically propelled vehicle to travel faster than ten miles an hour, and insisted that all such machines should be preceded by a man carrying a red flag (111). It was not until 1894 that motor-cars first appeared on British roads, and then only in small numbers. Their cost was high; and the difficulties that faced the early motorists were enough to daunt all but the most enthusiastic. Today we have almost forgotten how real and how serious those

116   A motor-car of 1910

117   A motor omnibus of 1904 (Orion type)

difficulties were. The horse-loving inhabitants of Great Britain did not take kindly to the new invention. Motorists were accused of ruining the countryside with their noise and fumes, of frightening horses (which they undoubtedly did), and of endangering human life. Magistrates viewed them with the deepest suspicion; horsemen of all kinds detested them; and some innkeepers even refused to allow motors to be put up in their yards.

The cars themselves were awkward looking and far from beautiful (10, 116). They were "horseless carriages" in form as well as in name, built on much the same lines as an ordinary carriage, but with an engine in front replacing the shafts. They were slow and unreliable: they constantly broke down, often in inconvenient places. One of the favourite jokes of the period concerned the supposed comments of their rival, the horse, when he was called upon to tow one of these stranded monsters. Nevertheless, despite ridicule and unpopularity, the motor-car had come to stay; and these pioneer vehicles were the first swallows of a spring that was soon to awaken the derelict roads of Britain to a new and vigorous life.

A great step forward was taken in 1896 when, by the Locomotive Highways Act, the hated red flag was abolished and the speed limit was raised to fourteen miles an hour. We should not now consider this a very dashing pace; and, even in those days, most cars were capable of doing better. But the Act showed that Parliament was at last beginning to take the new invention seriously, and made it possible for Britain to compete with other countries in motor-car production. From that time more and more cars were seen upon the roads. New designs and improvements were introduced. In 1897 the Automobile Club of Great Britain and Ireland was founded; and this club, by the trials it held, did much to foster the production of cars that were at once faster, more reliable and more comfortable.

In 1903 the speed limit was again raised, this time to twenty miles an hour; while, during the same year, the first experimental motor-bus went trundling down a London street. Eight years later, on October 25th, 1911, the last horse-drawn London bus made its last journey, and thenceforward only motor-buses were used in the capital (117). Across the Atlantic, Henry Ford, who in 1893 drove the first, and for a long time the only, car in

Detroit, was founding his great factory. In Oxford in 1912 a cycle-maker named William Morris—now better known as Lord Nuffield—was turning his attention to the production of motor-cars. The famous Rolls-Royce car, the joint work of Henry Royce and Charles Rolls, appeared in 1903; and there were many other mechanical newcomers. By 1913 Mr. Lloyd George could announce, at the International Road Congress, that England then had 220,000 licensed motor vehicles—twice as many as any Continental country, though only one-third as many as the United States.

The motor-car and the motor-bus heralded a revolution that their inventors probably had never foreseen. They made remote places accessible, brought new life to inns and country towns, and everywhere altered the pattern of life. People began to travel more for pleasure and to think less of distance; and thousands found employment in the great factories of Birmingham, Coventry and Derby, or in motor sales-rooms, garages and wayside filling-stations. But the advance of the car and the great increase of traffic also created their own problems. Most of the existing major roads had to be widened; and in the years following 1906 many new highways were built, including by-pass roads. In time, the British road-system became one of the finest in the world; but this proud position was not achieved without some sacrifices. Very often the motorist's gain was the countryman's loss. Arterial roads, driving their straight course across country, cut off pieces of fields and gardens, destroyed lovely old lanes, and swept away trees that had given shade and beauty for centuries. Frequently, too, a crop of jerry-built villas and shops sprang up in their wake, spread out in hideous "ribbon development", increasing traffic congestion on the very roads that had been specially built to lessen it. Such changes in the landscape may be convenient, but they are seldom beautiful. We must reckon them as part of the heavy price we pay for twentieth-century comfort and speed.

Chapter XI

TRANSPORT: SEA AND AIR

WHILE on land the steam locomotive was steadily advancing in importance and power, the steamship was furthering man's conquest of the sea. A brief account has been given of the advent of the steamship in *Everyday Things*, Vol. III. We must remember the pioneer work of Hulls and the Marquis de Jouffroy during the eighteenth century and, in Scotland, of that of William Symington and Henry Bell with his *Comet*, rivalled in America by John Fitch—who invented screw propellers—and by Robert Fulton, whose *Cleremont* ran on the Hudson River. Steamers had crossed the Atlantic and sailed to the Far East; and at the beginning of our period iron ships had been constructed; while the screw propeller had appeared with the *Great Britain* in 1845. Long before this, however, Francis Pettit Smith had built a steam screw launch, the *Francis Smith*, at Wapping; and the Admiralty adopted the screw for some ships after a tug-of-war trial in April, 1845, between the paddle-sloop *Alecto* and the screw-sloop *Rattler*, in which the latter proved victorious.

From that moment the iron ship reigned supreme among steamers, and the screw propeller came more and more into use. In 1858 the *Great Eastern* was launched with both paddle-wheels and a screw propeller, her makers hoping by this means to secure her against all difficulties (119). But, despite this precaution, she was never a success. When she was launched, she stuck upon the ways from November to January, and, on her journey down the English Channel, a boiler burst and killed six men. She was intended for the Australian passenger trade; but, notwithstanding her great size—practically six times greater than any other vessel then afloat—and the many costly improvements embodied in her construction, she never carried anything like her full complement of passengers. A rumour spread that she was haunted by a ghost who made unexplained tapping noises in all sorts of weather. These sounds had probably a natural origin; but repeated investigations failed to solve the

118 *The Orient*, built in 1878 for the Australian passenger service of the Orient Line. 9,500 tons, 15 knots

119 The *Great Eastern*, 1853–88, designed by Scott Russell and Isambard K. Brunel, the Great Western Railway engineer. She cost £640,000 and was 700 feet long, 32,000 tons displacement

mystery. When the ship was broken up in 1888, the skeleton of a riveter was found in her bilge, with a riveter's hammer beside him, and all who believed in the ghost story felt that they had proved their point. However that may be, the *Great Eastern* was not a success as a passenger ship; and in 1865 she began a new career as a cable-layer(120).

Before the invention of the electric telegraph, the only method of communication between one place and another was by letter, messenger or wooden signalling devices on hills and coastal eminences. The first public telegraph in England appeared in 1844; and four years later a cable was stretched under New York Harbour by Morse, whose celebrated code of dots and dashes is now generally employed. The first British cable was laid between Dover and Calais in 1850; and, in 1858, an attempt was made to bridge the Atlantic by this means(8). It was not successful; but even so, enough had been achieved to show that such a method of communication was feasible.

120　On board the *Great Eastern*. Searching for a fault after recovery of the Cable from the bed of the Atlantic, about 1866

From a contemporary drawing by Robert Dudley

In 1865, therefore, the shore end of an Atlantic cable was landed at Valentia, in South-West Ireland, and the *Great Eastern* set out across the ocean with the rest of it on board(120). As faults were discovered they were remedied, and messages reporting progress were sent home. But when the ship was already two-thirds of the way over and success seemed certain, silence fell. The cable had broken, and all attempts to find the severed end proved fruitless. For a time the enterprise had to be abandoned; but, in the following

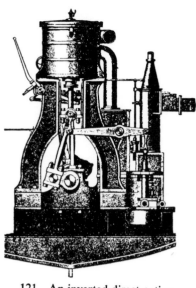

121   An inverted direct-acting marine engine

year, a new cable was successfully laid down, and the broken one recovered and completed.

The early marine engines were cumbersome affairs; they had many complications and, with their low steam pressure, worked slowly. About the middle of the century the compound engine was introduced, by which the steam was used successively in a small high-pressure and larger low-pressure cylinder. This was still further developed into a triple-expansion type with three—and occasionally four—cylinders which gave a more economical working with the triple use of steam. The cylinders were placed high above the screw shaft, on to which they worked downwards, so that the engine is called inverted direct-acting(121). This, with the Stephenson link motion valve gear familiar in railway engines, held the field as a standard type for many years, and is still widely used. The turbine type is not often employed for cargo steamers, since it is very expensive to construct.

On the other hand, the internal combustion engine began to come more and more into marine use at the close of the nineteenth century; for it has the great advantage of requiring neither a very large space for boilers nor a big staff of stokers.

Consequently small river boats are now usually motor driven, as well as coasting vessels and even great passenger liners. There are several types of motors—among them the Diesel, in which the explosion takes place by intensive compression without a spark. They are started by the use of highly compressed air. Special arrangements are made to obtain slow-running engines to minimise vibration. Some chief engineers today have worked all their lives on motor-driven vessels without experience of steam. There is also a Diesel-electric system; and even auxiliary apparatus, such as the winches, capstan, etc., is all electrically driven. In fact, the development of electricity in ships had been a marked feature of the latter part of the nineteenth century; and the electricity room of a large liner is big enough and supplies enough power for a fair-sized town.

The *Great Eastern* never got on to the Australian run; but by contrast we show *The Orient*, built twenty years later, in 1879, for the Orient Line (118). She was specially designed for the Australian passenger trade, on which she ran for over thirty years. She was the first ship to be lit by electric light, and the first in the Australian service to be fitted with refrigeration. When launched she was the largest vessel afloat after the *Great Eastern*, and had much of the outward appearance of a modern steamer; but she was still equipped with four square-rigged masts, replaced by two pole-masts, and a single funnel in 1897. She was built of iron, 445 feet long, having a beam of $46\frac{1}{4}$ feet, was of 9,500 tons displacement, and driven by a single set of three-cylinder engines of 5,400 horse-power, with one screw, giving an average speed of 15 knots. She could reach Australia without coaling on the way.

The next stage in the steamship's history was the building of steel ships, which first appeared in British waters in 1879, when the *Rotomahana* was built at Dumbarton. In 1881 the Cunard Line launched the first steel liner, the *Servia*, which was also the first of their ships to be fitted with electric light. In 1899 the dimensions of the *Great Eastern* were exceeded by the building of the *Oceanic*, 705 feet long.

Then, in 1884, a new and important invention for marine engines was introduced by Sir Charles Parsons. This was the steam turbine, an invention by which a jet of steam turns a number of blades in a rotating cylinder, in much the same way as the wind turns the sails of a windmill. The device was first tried out in a small experimental boat, the *Turbinia*, which in 1897 attained a speed of 34½ knots. To begin with, it was used mainly on yachts and small vessels; but, in 1901, the *King Edward*, a passenger ship, was fitted with turbine engines; and four years later they were used in the ocean-liner *Carmania*, to which they gave a speed of 22 knots. From that time, turbines were generally used for high-speed ships; and this form of engine is still employed in all fast-moving steam-driven liners, and in the destroyers and larger ships of the Royal Navy.

Although steam was destined to supersede sail, it did not do so completely for many years. While steamers were being built and perfected, the sailing-ship was not only widely used but also gained in speed and beauty. A full-rigged ship is one of the most beautiful things in the world; and in Victorian times these lovely vessels still crowded the waters, and some famous shipping lines, like the Black Ball of Liverpool and the Loch Line of Glasgow, employed no other form of craft. Rival companies built steamers and sailing-ships side by side; and, for nearly a century, there was strong competition between the different types of vessel. The last great sailing-ship was built at Greenock as recently as 1906; and right up to 1939 a few of these graceful bird-like craft were still regularly engaged in bringing wool, grain, and other non-perishable goods from Australia and elsewhere.

In the early days of steam, sailing-ships often proved far more economical than steamers, and as fast or faster. The first steamers consumed vast quantities of coal. A disproportionate amount of space was taken up in carrying fuel, or long and expensive halts had to be made at coaling-stations on the way. Wind-driven ships laboured under no such disadvantages; and it was not until the steamer's speed had been greatly increased, and her running costs reduced, that the long battle between sail and steam was finally decided in favour of the steam-ship.

The most famous nineteenth-century sailing-ship was the clipper. This was a comparatively small vessel, usually of about 1,500 tons, specially designed for high speeds and the rapid carrying of valuable cargoes over long distances. She was much faster than any of the larger sailing-ships, and was built with a peculiar fineness of line towards the stern that enabled her to move with great rapidity. In their heyday, the clippers were used mainly in the China tea trade. Tea was still rather an expensive luxury in mid-Victorian times, and the first of the new season's crop fetched very high prices in London. The ships belonging to the various companies therefore raced each other every year across the ocean with their precious load, every man on board, from the captain down to the least of the crew, doing his utmost to bring his ship home first, as much for the honour of the victory as for the rewards distributed by the owners. No more lovely sight has ever been seen than such exquisite, fine-lined vessels as *Ariel*, *Thermopylae*, *Taeping* or *Cutty Sark* racing at full speed through the water with all their canvas set; and it is not surprising that reports of their progress should have been received with great excitement at home. Their exploits were chronicled in the newspapers; and the fortunes of the various ships were as closely watched and wagered upon as those of any racehorse or famous racing motorist today.

The *Cutty Sark* is perhaps the best known to us of all these ships because she had the good luck to be perserved, and is now on public exhibition. She was built in 1869 for Captain John Willis; and in her prime, given a good wind, she could outsail most contemporary steamers. Eleven or twelve knots was then a very fair speed for a steamship; the *Cutty Sark* could do 17 or 17½ knots at her best; and, even so, she was not as fast as the *Lightning*, the *Taeping*, and one or two other tea-clippers.

Although, during the Victorian age, she came into her full perfection, the sailing-ship was now doomed. The clippers did not long survive the opening of the Suez Canal; for they could not use that short cut to the East, and steamers could. One by one they disappeared from the tea-routes, some to work in the Australian wool trade, some to become coal-hulks, and others to be broken up for scrap. The larger sailing-vessels survived a little longer. Between 1918 and 1939 many of them were still regularly used by Captain Gustav Erikson of Marieham in the grain trade; and one at least, the *Pamir*, sailed until 1957. His *Herzogin Cecilie*, alas, was wrecked off Bolt Tail, South Devon, in a fog in 1936. We well remember the noble appearance, one evening in 1936, of the brig *Passat*, seen from the deck of a modern vessel in Swedish waters, outlined against the sunset with all her sails set. She was returning from Australia, as useful and efficient in her old age as ever she had been in the great days of sail.

While all these advances in transport were being made on land and sea, experiments of various kinds were being attempted in the air. The earliest form of aerial flight was in balloons, which had been successfully flown by the Montgolfier brothers in France as far back as 1783. The great disadvantage of balloons, however, was that they could not be steered and were at the mercy of every gust of wind. Inventors, therefore, turned their attention to finding some method of controlling these new vessels, and for many years experiments in the production of dirigible airships went on. The earliest were worked by hand; and, even in 1870, we hear of an airship 119 feet long, with a revolving screw which was hand-driven, the ship being rowed through the air, at about eight miles an hour, by a crew of eight men.

In 1852 a great advance was made by Henri Giffard, a French engineer, who constructed an airship driven by a screw-propelled steam engine. This engine was specially designed for aerial flights, being extremely light; and with it Giffard succeeded in moving his ship at a speed of about five or six miles an hour. Ten years before, an even more interesting experiment had been made, when Samuel Henson built a model monoplane driven by steam. This machine, known as "the aerial steam carriage", was much derided at the time. It never passed beyond the model stage; but its trials were important landmarks in the history of aviation; for they showed, for the first time, the possibility of power-propelled aeroplanes, as distinct from gas-filled airships or balloons.

In 1871 a German named Otto Lilienthal began to make a serious study of the flight of birds. From his boyhood he had been fascinated by the sight of their effortless movements, and particularly by those of a colony of storks that nested on the roofs of his village. He noticed how easily they travelled and how they made use of every current of air; how they could shoot along at great speeds, or remain stationary for long periods, even in a wind. He was convinced that, if only the principles of their flight were rightly understood, it should be possible for man to imitate them; and he devoted many years to the study of this problem. In 1889 he published the result of his researches in a book called *Bird Flight as a Basis of Aviation.*

Two years later, he passed from study to personal experiment. He built a glider that consisted of two outstretched planes covered with cotton twill, stretched upon a willow frame. Between the wings there was a space through which the inventor thrust his head and shoulders, while holding firmly to the sides with either hand. By running to give himself momentum, and having leapt from a height of 20 feet, he managed to glide for about 80 feet. At the same time, he learnt to alter direction and overcome the effect of air currents by moving his legs and swinging his body to one side or the other. Later, he built another machine with two planes, one above the other; and with this he achieved much longer glides. He then constructed a motor-driven glider; and he was just about to begin testing it when he was killed while gliding at Stollen in 1896.

Others, in the meantime, were experimenting along the same lines. In England Percy Pilcher used a glider with a wheeled undercarriage, the first of its type. Like Lilienthal, he was designing a power-driven machine when he, too, fell to his death in 1899, the first Englishman to perish during an aerial flight. In America the famous Wright brothers began gliding in 1900 near Kitty Hawk, in North Carolina. They used a biplane, like their predecessors; but when gliding they lay along the lower wing, instead of hanging downwards from the framework. This reduced the air resistance; and by 1901 they were making flights of more than 600 feet at a time. Finally, in 1903, they built a machine with a twelve-horse-power four-cylinder motor, which was to become famous in history as the first man-carrying, power-driven aeroplane ever successfully flown.

On December 17th of that year, in cold and rather windy weather, the preliminary tests took place. The aeroplane rose easily from its supporting trolley, made a short straight flight lasting about twelve seconds, and came down again without difficulty. Orville Wright was the pilot; and as witnesses of this epoch-making event there were, besides the inventors, only five other men. Scientists and inventors all over the world recognised the great importance of that day's doings. But to the ordinary man or woman it was just a curious item of news which he or she read at breakfast.

Yet few events have heralded greater changes in peace and in war than that short twelve-second flight in rural America. From that day, the existence of the aeroplane as a means of transport was established; and all that remained was to improve and perfect it. The early machines were not capable of long, sustained flights. When Henry Farman flew for about two minutes and covered a little more than a mile in 1908, it was considered a great achievement. Wilbur Wright's first flight over France, in the same year, lasted only one minute and forty-seven seconds. Gradually, however, the staying-power of the aeroplane increased. In a later test, the Wrights flew for more than two hours and carried a passenger at a height of 400 feet; and then, in 1909, Louis Blériot astonished the world by crossing the English Channel in a single flight that lasted thirty-seven minutes.

By this time aviation schools were springing up. The world's first flying-meeting was held at Rheims in 1909; and to it flocked enthusiasts from every country. In 1910 the *Daily Mail* offered a prize of £10,000 for a race from London to Manchester, which was won by a French aviator, Louis Paulhan. During the same year, C. S. Rolls flew from Dover to Calais and back again without coming down, and Robert Lorraine crossed the Irish Sea. In 1911, Beaumont (Lieutenant Conneau of the French Navy) won a round-Britain race extending over 1,010 miles, and another of 815 miles between Paris and Rome. At the same time the first mail-carrying flight was made between Hendon and Windsor; and eight years later, in 1919, two Englishmen, John Alcock and Arthur Whitten-Brown, crossed the Atlantic, 1,890 miles, in a single eastward non-stop flight of sixteen hours.

Today the aeroplane is used everywhere for defence and attack in war, for commerce, mail-carrying, travel, and a dozen other peaceful purposes. So accustomed have we become to the sight and sound of giant machines roaring over our heads that we scarcely trouble to look up. Yet there is no one over sixty years old who cannot remember a time when there were no aeroplanes. Nor is there any one over fifty who cannot recall the days when these strange contrivances seemed a fascinating prodigy to all who beheld them.

Chapter XII

AMUSEMENTS AND HOLIDAYS

MID-VICTORIAN amusements were mainly of a simple and cheerful kind. People relied upon themselves for their own entertainment far more than we do now; and, as a rule, they did it very successfully. Visits to the theatre, the circus, or the seaside(138, 141–3) were the highlights of the year; but the rest of the Victorian family's leisure was filled with amusements that were, perhaps, all the more enjoyable because they were of their own making.

In a large family—and families were usually large—there was nearly always something interesting to do. The children had their own games and occupations in the nursery, and if they had only a few playthings and hardly any mechanical toys, they managed very well with what they had. Downstairs in the drawing-room their elder sisters read, embroidered, and made curious objects with shells or wax that were then very much admired. They also sketched, or played the piano, or sang. Reading aloud was a favourite occupation in some families. The nature of the book chosen depended largely upon the age of the person reading. If it were a parent, some serious, instructive, and rather dull work might be taken from the shelves; but younger people had plenty of novels and illustrated magazines at their disposal. At the beginning of our period, novel-reading was still often considered a waste of time, if not actually harmful, and every book was carefully inspected by mother or governess before it was allowed in a young girl's hands.

Those who could afford it entertained a good deal, just as they do today; but, in that decorous and precise age, there was considerably more formality than is usual today. Visiting friends was generally a lengthy business which involved the transport of much luggage; for it was not uncommon for guests to remain in their friends' houses for a couple of months or longer. A short stay would have been considered scarcely worth while; and week-end visits did not come into fashion until the last years of the nineteenth century.

194

122 A dinner party, 1883. The ladies withdraw
By George du Maurier

123 Sunday morning Church Parade in Hyde Park, 1876
By N. W. Ridley

124   Packing up for the family holiday, 1867
By John Leech

Dinner-parties (122) were very formal gatherings, with long and heavy meals of many courses, followed by music in the drawing-room which the daughters of the house, or the guests themselves, supplied. To ensure success in this form of entertaining, the hostess had to be well versed in the social order of precedence, so that her visitors might go in to dinner in the due order of their rank. Great trouble also had to be taken to pair them off suitably, each lady going to the dining-room on the arm of the gentleman selected for her, and taking her allotted seat at his side.

At the end of the meal, the women withdrew to the drawing-room (122) while the men remained behind to drink port and gossip until their host invited them to "join the ladies". In mid-Victorian times, when dinner was eaten early, tea was served after it, but, as the century wore on and the dinner-hour became later and later, this custom gave place to separate tea-parties at four or five o'clock.

Sometimes cards were played during the evening, though this

196

125   Belgravia out-of-doors
From "Bird's-eye Views of Society", by Richard Doyle

was frowned upon by very religious families. Picquet, loo and whist were the customary games, for bridge was hardly known then. Usually, however, a few songs and a great deal of conversation was considered amusement enough for an evening, which ended with the arrival of the guests' carriages to take them home.

Balls were more elaborate functions, whether they took place in a private house or the local Assembly Rooms. No young girl went to them (or, indeed, anywhere else in public) without a chaperone, her mother or some other married woman, beside whom she sat on a gilded chair until some young man came to ask her to dance. After each dance, her partner was expected to return her to her guardian's care; and to dance more than three times with one man was considered extremely forward; and if any girl was rash enough to do so, it was expected that her engagement would be announced very shortly afterwards.

After a dinner or a ball, calls were made by the guests to

126   An August picnic, 1869

127   Archery, 1865
By John Leech

thank the hostess for her hospitality. Calling was a very important feature of social life, and much time was devoted to it, especially by women. Newcomers to a neighbourhood had to wait until the established residents called upon them before they could make any move in local society. Sometimes they had to wait for a considerable time; for, in some districts, a practice known as "summering and wintering a newcomer" obtained, which meant that no one approached them for nearly a year. If the newcomer was a bachelor, the male head of the resident family called upon him. Otherwise the wife left her own and her husband's cards, and either drove straight on or, if she went in, stayed only for a very short time. Soon afterwards the newcomer returned the call in the same formal manner; and thereafter the two families were considered to be acquaintances.

Luncheon parties did not become usual until the beginning of the twentieth century; but summer garden parties were very popular. Croquet(140) was a favourite entertainment at such gatherings, and so were archery contests, for archery was

199

considered a graceful sport in which women as well as men could join (127). Lawn tennis did not come into fashion until the 'seventies, when women's clothes were better suited to it; and even then it was a very gentle game (91). Outdoor sports, like hunting, shooting, fishing, riding, cricket and football, were mainly for men; though women rode to hounds and shared in boating expeditions, picnics (126), and other summer delights organised by their husbands and brothers.

Cricket had been popular for many years before the opening of our period; but football was only just coming into favour. Played at an earlier period as a rough country game without any firmly fixed rules, by 1801 it had fallen into disrepute. Then the public schools revived it on their playing-fields. Rugger came into existence at Rugby, where, in 1823, William Webb Ellis first took the ball into his arms and ran with it; and Soccer was established in 1863, when the Football Association was founded and definite rules were for the first time drawn up. Country people still played some of the old games, like stoolball, trap-ball, or knurr and spell; but they gradually died out as the century advanced, and by the beginning of King Edward's reign they had almost all disappeared.

Eighteenth-century London had had many pleasure-gardens, of which Vauxhall and Ranelagh were the most famous. But gradually their popularity had declined, until, in 1850, only two were left—the Royal Cremorne Gardens at Chelsea (128) and Rosherville Gardens at Gravesend. Here displays of all sorts were provided—fireworks, military tournaments, balloon ascents, dancing, marionettes, and a host of other amusements. Cremorne had originally been the private garden of Lord Cremorne's riverside house; and, to the end, it was a pleasant rural-looking place, full of green lawns, trees and flowers. But, during its last years, it became extremely rowdy. Quieter people were afraid to go to visit it; and there were constant complaints from nearby residents about the nightly uproar. As a result partly of these complaints, and partly of a shocking accident in 1874 when a balloonist was killed, Cremorne was closed in 1877. So unpleasant had it at length become that nobody regretted it; and now houses and streets cover its verdant lawns and shady dells.

One of the great Christmas treats for children was the visit to

128　An evening at Cremorne Gardens, Chelsea, in the 1860s

129　Wombwell's Menagerie, about 1860

130 Archery, 1870   131 Roller-skating, 1875   132 Golf clothes, 1889
133 Croquet, 1861   134 Cricket dress, 1890

130–4 Sports Dress over Thirty Years

the Pantomime, with its marvellous transformation scene, its songs, dances and jokes, and, of course, the closing Harlequinade. Originally the Harlequinade had been the principal part of the performance, graced by a lovely Columbine, a mysterious Harlequin, a doddering Pantaloon and a jovial Clown. But gradually other attractions were added to prolong the show. In course of time, the Harlequinade sank to the position of a mere comic turn, for which those with long journeys to make or trains to catch could not always wait. Today we hardly ever see it; and in Victorian times it was already declining; while the preliminary Pantomime was coming into its full glory. This and the Circus were the crowning delights of Christmas, and great was the excitement in nurseries and schoolrooms as Boxing Day, the opening date of the Pantomime season, drew near.

Going to the theatre was then the chief amusement of its kind; for music-halls(137), though they were extremely popular, were not considered fit places for women and children. Theatres

135   The "Gods"—a gallery audience of 1895
By Maurice Greiffenhagen

203

were lit by gas; the better seats were upholstered in red plush, but those in the gallery were wooden, backless benches. But a little discomfort was not enough to keep the gallery patrons away(135). They came in their hundreds to express their approval or disapproval of the acting, and to see the ladies in the stalls and boxes down below(136). A Victorian gala night at a theatre was a very gay affair, what with the lights and the music, the pretty frocks and rustling skirts, and the richly coloured stage displays; and usually they ended with the handing-up of dozens of lovely bouquets brought by admirers of the favourite actresses.

This was a great age in the history of acting, and of that lighter type of entertainment called vaudeville. Crowds flocked every night in the season to see such magnificent performers as Samuel Phelps, Henry Irving or Ellen Terry, or less serious, but no less great, musical stars—Kate Vaughan, George Grossmith, Nellie Farren, and many others. Straight plays, musical comedies, burlesques and vaudeville shows were all extremely popular; and towards the end of the century began the long series of comic operas composed in partnership by W. S. Gilbert and Arthur Sullivan, still almost as well beloved by audiences today as they were when they first appeared at the Savoy Theatre in London eighty years ago.

Music-halls at the beginning of our period were rather rough-and-ready establishments, where a genial chairman presided over the show and introduced each turn to an audience that smoked and drank as it watched the various comedians, dancers and singers. The patrons were all men. No one in mid-Victorian times would have dreamt of taking his wife or sister there, and indeed some of the jokes and songs were scarcely fit for a feminine audience. But as the century wore on music-halls improved enormously, both in comfort and in the nature of the performance they provided; and by the end of Queen Victoria's reign great stars like Vesta Tilley, Marie Lloyd, Dan Leno and George Robey were delighting packed houses everywhere in London and the big towns.

It was in the music-hall that the cinematograph, or the biograph as it was then called, first regularly appeared as a short turn at the end of the ordinary performance. No one seems quite certain who first invented this new form of entertainment. Thomas Edison, the inventor of the telephone, is usually given the credit for it; but Edward Muybridge, a Californian photographer, appears to have produced the first moving picture. This he showed to Edison, who was immediately interested, though even he had little idea of the heights to which it would eventually rise in the entertainment world. He thought of it chiefly as an addition to his own "talking-machine". Others in England, France and America were working on the same notion at the same time. As early as 1890, a man called Friese-Greene demonstrated something akin to the cinematograph at a meeting of the Bath Photographic Society; while the first film ever shown to a paying audience was displayed in New York on May 20th, 1895.

Nine months later, on February 20th, 1896, a British audience made history by paying to see a short display of films given by two French brothers named Lumière in the Regent Street Polytechnic, in London. Later on, the music-halls began to show short films. The early films were very jerky, and so covered with spots that a black rain seemed to descend upon the actors. They lasted only for a few minutes; and at first depicted simple incidents— the arrival of a train at a station, horses galloping, or a rough sea dashing against the shore. But the figures did actually move, however jerkily, and sometimes it was possible to see a person one knew descending from a train or moving across the screen.

Later on comic films became very popular, with comedians throwing custard-pies at each other or playing practical jokes

136   The dress circle, 1869
By John Leech

137   The Lord Raglan Music-Hall, 1857

upon unsuspecting victims; and these were followed by thrilling Wild West stories in which the heroine endured untold perils from fire, flood and Red Indians, while the pianist played loud and exciting music. The music was necessary because the early films were, of course, completely silent. The "talkies" did not come in until January, 1929. During the first years of King Edward VII's reign, to enjoy "the pictures" was considered slightly vulgar. But it was not at all an expensive form of amusement. In those happy days it was possible to go to "the pictures" for threepence; the best seats often cost only sixpence; and picture-houses where a shilling was charged were "palaces" indeed.

One of the pioneer exhibitions of cinematography in London was a show run by Henry Iles, which was known as "Hales' Tours of the World". Iles rented a large shop in Oxford Street and fitted it up like the inside of a railway carriage. The screen was at the far end of the carriage; and on it were shown films taken from the back or front of a train, to give the effect of a railway journey. Noises like the sounds of an engine, the grinding of wheels and the blast of a guard's whistle added to the illusion. This show, for which sixpence was charged, was very popular, and was repeated in several of the larger provincial towns.

Empty shops, fitted with tip-up seats, were quite often used in the early twentieth century for shows that lasted about an hour. But, from about 1906, special cinematograph-theatres began to be built, and these multiplied very rapidly. The films improved greatly as time went on; the houses became more luxurious and more expensive; and gradually a regular "film-public" came into being. Even so, many who had promoted such enterprises lost their money; and it was a long time before the proprietors of ordinary theatres understood how dangerous a rival the film industry was rapidly becoming.

An exciting annual event in the life of every Victorian family was their visit to the seaside. Almost everyone who could afford it spent a month or a fortnight by the sea, and those who could not manage so long a holiday went there for two or three days. But this habit was still comparatively new at the beginning of our period. Rich people had always travelled for pleasure; but, until the middle of the eighteenth century, they went to inland spas rather than to the coast. Sea-bathing(138, 143) was not at all popular until doctors discovered that it was good for health, and George III made it fashionable by visiting Weymouth every year. Even then, it was chiefly the aristocratic and the well-to-do who patronised the coastal watering-places.

138   Bathing girls, showing the bathing-machine "Modesty Hood", 1861
By John Leech

It was the coming of the railways that made regular seaside trips possible for everyone. By 1848 there were already 5,000 miles of railway track in England; and the various companies that served the coast encouraged holidaymakers by issuing excursion tickets at reduced rates for day trips and for family parties. Margate, Brighton, Blackpool, Scarborough, and a host of other towns were now filled up every year by visitors from London and all the big centres. Their streets were thronged with crowds of sightseers and shopgazers; in the height of the season their beaches were black with parents, nurses, and children, who bathed, paddled, dug in the sands, rode upon donkeys, collected seaweed and starfish, or simply sat in the sun. The lodging-houses were crammed with visitors; and so were the hotels, though these were far fewer and less luxurious than they are now. Rich people rented houses on the seafront and brought their own servants with them.

It was usual for the whole family to go away together; and their joint preparations sometimes extended over two or three weeks(124). No one then dreamt of "travelling light", with just a suitcase or two for each person. Indeed, when we remember the amount of space taken up by crinolines and bustles, starched petticoats and ruffled frocks, it is obvious that this would have been quite out of the question. Mountains of trunks, baskets and holdalls(139) were piled on the roof of the waiting cab; and to these were added such cumbersome articles as a cradle or cot for the baby, and a flat tin bath for use in the bathroomless lodging-houses of those days. Sunshades, umbrellas, shawls, fans, sketching-materials, embroidery-frames, and toys for the children had all to be got in somehow; and, last, there were packages of food to be eaten on the railway, where restaurant-cars were as yet unknown.

Most journeys, of course, were made by train; but if a London family went to Margate, they might elect to travel all the way by steamer, which meant a pleasant six- or seven-hour voyage down the Thames and round the Kentish coast.

Once the holiday-makers had arrived, the amusements they found awaiting them varied according to the resort they had chosen. In the small, "select" resorts, there was not very much to do besides walking, sketching, boating, going on picnics(126)

or expeditions and, of course, bathing(138, 143). Most seaside
towns had a reading-room and a circulating library, good shops,
a concert-hall, and perhaps a theatre. For the serious-minded
there were sometimes lectures or scientific demonstrations; for
the energetic, there were archery contests(127), riding, bowls,
croquet(140) and, towards the end of the century, lawn tennis
(91). When it rained, the visitors had to fall back upon an
occasional concert, and such home-made amusements as embroidery, reading and visiting friends.

The larger and more crowded resorts were very different.
The Victorians, in their normal workaday lives, were quiet and
rather sober people; but, when they left home, a good many of
them seem to have welcomed incessant bustle and clatter. The
popular seaside resorts resounded with music. German bands
played on the seafront and outside the principal hotels. Itinerant
fiddlers, cornet-players, bagpipers and organ-grinders infested
the side roads. The beaches and promenades, at all hours, were
filled with surging crowds whose talk and laughter mingled with
the barking of dogs, the shouting of children, and the cries of

139   Victorian luggage
By John Leech
209

140   Croquet, 1867
By John Leech

women selling eels, mussels, shrimps, flowers or sweetmeats. Travelling showmen and circuses visited the seaside towns and advertised their presence by noisy processions, with drummers, trumpeters, and rumbling caravans. Dancing bears and performing monkeys delighted the children; and old and young flocked to see the Punch-and-Judy shows and the nigger minstrels on the beach.

From about 1858, "nigger minstrels" were very popular in England. They came originally from America and performed at first in London. But they soon spread to the seaside; and, before long, there was scarcely any large holiday town without at least one troupe of black-faced musicians. Dressed in brightly-coloured tail-coats, striped trousers, huge spotted bow-ties, and straw hats with coloured ribbons, they cracked jokes, sang popular ballads and plantation songs, and played banjos and concertinas. For forty years or so, they had it all their own way; and then, about the beginning of King Edward's reign, the pierrot troupes appeared. Their performance was lighter and aimed (though not always successfully) at a higher standard of wit and sophistication. Unlike the nigger minstrels, they included women, and appealed more directly to the Edwardian taste for elegance. Slowly but surely they supplanted the nigger minstrels in popular favour. But right up to the end of our period it was still possible to see Uncle Bones and his men at most of our seaside towns.

Another great attraction was the pier, which, during Victorian times, developed up from a simple landing-stage of tarred wood or iron into a magnificent promenade, with its pavilion and concert-hall, its sideshows and little shops, with which we are familiar today. The famous Chain Pier at Brighton was built in 1823 to allow passengers from Dieppe to land without the inconvenience of being carried ashore in small boats, or on the shoulders of longshoremen. It was, in fact, intended for use rather than for pleasure; but visitors were encouraged to walk on it by the presence of a few green-painted benches, a sundial, a weighing-machine and a *camera obscura*. There were also one or two booths where mineral waters could be bought; and now and then the whole pier was illuminated at night. Margate pier started in much the same way. Originally there was a jetty for the use of boats; and, when this was damaged by a storm in 1808, it was rebuilt on a more elaborate plan, with a gallery in which a band played on fine days. In 1812, someone had the daring notion of charging one penny for admission to their pier;

141   Brighton Promenade, 1879

but this so infuriated inhabitants and visitors that there was a serious riot.

By the beginning of Queen Victoria's reign, the idea that piers might be amusement centres, rather than landing-stages or not, was already well established. All through the following years, progressive town councils were busy erecting these long seaward promenades, which grew more and more elaborate as time went on. In 1896, the old Chain Pier at Brighton was swept away by a storm; but, long before that time, a second and more modern structure had been built; while nearly every other seaside town of any size had at least one pier, and sometimes two or three.

Of all the pleasures that made the summer holiday memorable, the chief, in most people's estimation, was sea-bathing. But

142   Bathing-dress,
1885

this, in Victorian times, was not quite the lighthearted amusement that it has since become. There was no running down from hotel to beach in a bathrobe, no sun-bathing, or lying about on the sands in bathing-dresses after the dip. Everything had to be done in an orderly and decorous manner. Mixed bathing was nowhere allowed. Men and women occupied separate parts of the beach, and were not supposed to meet in the water. Boats were forbidden to approach within a certain distance of the ladies' bathing-place; and, if they did so, their owners were liable to a fine.

Bathing-clothes were also carefully regulated. Men were expected to cover their chests; and women were obliged to wear thick, cumbersome serge garments that muffled them completely from head to foot. Swathed in yards of wet serge, even a good swimmer could not hope to do much; and most feminine bathing of that time consisted chiefly of bobbing up and down in the water and splashing about within easy reach of the shore(138).

On the beach, when they wished to enter

the sea, women had to wait their turn for a bathing-machine, a sort of wooden cabin on wheels which was drawn right down to the water's edge by horses. On its seaward side, a sort of hood or canopy projected outwards and downwards over the water, completely screening the bather until she had actually taken the plunge. There was a bathing-woman in attendance, part of whose duty was to dip—in other words, to seize the bather as soon as she emerged and, for the good of her health, dip her forcibly two or three times(143).

The usual charge for a bathing-machine was sixpence or a shilling. This included its use for dressing and undressing, the services of the dipper, and a rather jerky ride up the beach afterwards to some place where the bather could conveniently alight. The chief disadvantages of these machines were that they were uncomfortable and rather draughty, and that their floors were often unpleasantly pebble-strewn. They vanished, however, when Victorian ideas of modesty changed; and, towards the end of the century, some daring individual conceived the idea of

143 Bathing-woman, 1861

213

sheltering bathers in small coloured tents. Meanwhile the custom of setting aside separate portions of the beach for men and for women was gradually undermined; and about 1900 Bexhill and a few other places took the bold step of permitting mixed bathing.

Bank Holidays, which brought the working-man down to the seaside, were unknown before 1871. In the early part of the nineteenth century, when the Industrial Revolution was in full swing, he was expected to toil without remission from Monday morning to Saturday night; and the same rule was observed by the majority of his employers. Weekly half-days were given only in a few trades. The only days of rest were Sundays and such customary holidays as had always been celebrated in particular districts. Even those were sadly diminished in the early days of the Industrial Revolution; for magistrates tended to suppress them, on the grounds that they encouraged idleness, rowdiness and damage to property.

Centuries before, in the Middle Ages, the great festivals of the Church were feasts as well as holy days; and, when once the people had attended morning service, they were free to spend the rest of the day in amusements. The Christmas holiday lasted twelve days; the parish Wakes often went on for nearly a week, and Whitsun, Easter, St. John's Day, Shrovetide and All Saints' were all celebrated with much rejoicing and complete freedom from all but necessary work. After the Reformation, less attention was paid to these religious anniversaries; but there were still a good many dates on which work ceased as a matter of course, and poor and rich alike gave themselves over to enjoyment.

With the coming of machines and the factory system, most of these festivals disappeared, at least as far as townspeople were concerned. Manufacturers and employers were too busy making money to trouble about holidays; and they saw no reason to allow their workers a privilege that they did not allow themselves. It was enough, they thought, if the working-man had regular work and a regular wage at the week-end. The result was, of course, that most artisans in towns were grossly overworked. Only a few enlightened employers understood that this was a bad state of affairs, both for the artisan himself and for the community at large.

Then, round about 1850, public opinion grew a little more progressive. The Factory Act of that year forbade the employment of women and children in any factory after two o'clock on Saturday afternoons; and what was thus made law for women and young people soon became the custom where men were concerned. Some old-fashioned employers disliked the new system intensely; but many others found it worked very well; and gradually the habit spread to trades that were not directly affected by the Factory Acts. Before long, the idea of a five-and-a-half-day week was generally accepted.

The Bank Holidays Act of 1871 had the effect of restoring to the people some of the ancient holidays that had been kept long ago as part of the great religious festivals of Easter, Whitsuntide, Lammas and Christmas. Good Friday and Christmas Day had never been working days, except during the Commonwealth; and now to these free days were added Easter Monday, Whit Monday, the first Monday in August and Boxing Day. Although they all fell immediately after or on religious feasts, the holidays themselves were given solely for business reasons, and were not connected in any way with the Church's calendar. This was an entirely new and perhaps not a very good idea; but the Act was important because it established the principle of a legal, rather than a customary, right to certain fixed holidays in every year.

From this point it was an easy step forward towards longer annual holidays, though most of these, even when they were allowed, had to be taken without pay. In the North of England it was (and still is) the custom to close the mills and foundries during the Wakes week while the machinery was overhauled. Most artisans in such towns saved throughout the year in order to be able to go to Blackpool, Morecambe, or some other local seaside place. In London, poor families often took a kind of working holiday by going hop-picking or fruit-gathering in Kent or elsewhere in the Home Counties. By the end of the nineteenth century, some employers allowed their workers a short time off with pay after twelve months' service; and today between eleven and twelve million working people enjoy a paid holiday every year. All these privileges—Saturday afternoons, Bank Holidays, annual holidays with or without pay—are now so much a part of our ordinary lives that we scarcely notice their existence; and we seldom spare a thought for the Victorian pioneers who did so much to improve our working lives. In this book we have often described the darker aspect of nineteenth-century England. Let us not forget the courageous men and women who helped to introduce the benefits of the modern Welfare State.

INDEX

INDEX

The numerals in **heavy type** denote the *figure numbers* of the illustrations

INDEX

221

INDEX

223

INDEX

INDEX